The Executive Guide to Understanding and Implementing Lean Six Sigma: The Financial Impact

Also available from ASQ Quality Press:

The Executive Guide to Understanding and Implementing Quality Cost Programs: Reduce Operating Expenses and Increase Revenue
Douglas Wood

The Executive Guide to Understanding and Implementing the Baldrige Criteria: Improve Revenue and Create Organizational Excellence
Denis Leonard, PhD and Mac McGuire, PhD

The Executive Guide to Understanding and Implementing Employee Engagement Programs: Expand Production Capacity, Increase Revenue, and Save Jobs
Pat Townsend and Joan Gebhardt

The Certified Manager of Quality/Organizational Excellence Handbook, Third Edition
Russell T. Westcott, editor

The Quality Improvement Handbook, Second Edition
ASQ Quality Management Division; John E. Bauer, Grace L. Duffy, and Russell T. Westcott, editors

The Executive Guide to Improvement and Change
G. Dennis Beecroft, Grace L. Duffy, and John W. Moran

Principles of Quality Costs: Principles, Implementation, and Use, Third Edition
Jack Campanella, editor

ANSI/ISO/ASQ Q10014-2006: Quality management—Guidelines for realizing financial and economic benefits
ANSI/ISO/ASQ

Lean Six Sigma for Healthcare: A Senior Leader Guide to Improving Cost and Throughput
Chip Caldwell, Jim Brexler, and Tom Gillem

Simplified Project Management for the Quality Professional: Managing Small and Medium-Size Projects
Russell T. Westcott

The Certified Six Sigma Green Belt Handbook
Roderick A. Munro, Matthew J. Maio, Mohamed B. Nawaz, and Daniel J. Zrymiak

To request a complimentary catalog of ASQ Quality Press publications, call 800-248-1946, or visit our Web site at http://qualitypress.asq.org.

The Executive Guide to Understanding and Implementing Lean Six Sigma: The Financial Impact

The ASQ Quality Management Division
Economics of Quality Book Series

Robert M. Meisel
Steven J. Babb
Steven F. Marsh
James P. Schlichting

ASQ Quality Press
Milwaukee, Wisconsin

American Society for Quality, Quality Press, Milwaukee 53203
© 2007 by ASQ
All rights reserved. Published 2007
Printed in the United States of America
13 12 11 10 09 08 07   5 4 3 2 1

Library of Congress Cataloging-in-Publication Data

The executive guide to understanding and implementing Lean Six Sigma: the financial
impact / Robert M. Meisel . . . [et al.].
    p. cm.—(The ASQ Quality management Division economics of quality book series)
    Includes bibliographical references and index.
    ISBN-13: 978-0-87389-711-2 (soft cover : alk. paper)
    ISBN-10: 0-87389-711-0 (soft cover : alk. paper)
    1. Business logistics—Management. 2. Six sigma (Quality control standard).
   I. Meisel, Robert M., 1948– II. American Society for Quality. Quality Management
Division.

   HD38.5.E99 2007
   658.4'013—dc22   2007001191

ISBN-13: 978-0-87389-711-2

Publisher: William A. Tony
Acquisitions Editor: Matt T. Meinholz
Project Editor: Paul O'Mara
Production Administrator: Randall Benson

ASQ Mission: The American Society for Quality advances individual, organizational,
and community excellence worldwide through learning, quality improvement, and
knowledge exchange.

Attention Bookstores, Wholesalers, Schools, and Corporations: ASQ Quality Press
books, videotapes, audiotapes, and software are available at quantity discounts with
bulk purchases for business, educational, or instructional use. For information,
please contact ASQ Quality Press at 800-248-1946, or write to ASQ Quality Press,
P.O. Box 3005, Milwaukee, WI 53201-3005.

To place orders or to request a free copy of the ASQ Quality Press Publications
Catalog, including ASQ membership information, call 800-248-1946. Visit our
Web site at www.asq.org or http://qualitypress.asq.org.

Printed in the United States of America

 Printed on acid-free paper

Quality Press
600 N. Plankinton Avenue
Milwaukee, Wisconsin 53203
Call toll free 800-248-1946
Fax 414-272-1734
www.asq.org
http://qualitypress.asq.org
http://standardsgroup.asq.org
E-mail: authors@asq.org

To Susan Meisel, Noris Babb, Loralee Marsh, and Mary Schlichting for reducing uncertainty and adding value in our lives.

Table of Contents

List of Figures and Tables . . . . *ix*

Introduction . . . . *xi*

Preface . . . . *xiii*

Chapter 1   Lean, Six Sigma, and Lean Six Sigma **1**

Background   1

Lean   2

Six Sigma   13

Lean versus Six Sigma or Lean and Six Sigma?   21

Preparing for Lean Six Sigma   23

Conclusion   25

Chapter 2   The Dollars and Sense of Improvement **27**

A Primer on Finance   29

How Improvement Contributes to Financials   31

Economics of the Seven Wastes   32

Cost of (Poor) Quality   35

Some Examples of Successful Improvement Initiatives   38

Some Guidelines on Balance Sheet Calculation   42

Chapter 3   Implementing Lean Six Sigma **45**

I'm Interested . . . Now What?   45

Getting Started   49

Growing Your Success   65

Sharing Your Successes   66

A Final Word   66

Appendix A   Cost of Quality Items **67**

**Appendix B   Case Study #1: Fort Wayne, Indiana—
Applying Lean Six Sigma to City Government** **71**

**Appendix C   Case Study #2: The Bank of America/
FleetBoston Merger—Ensuring Customer Delight with
Lean Six Sigma** **75**

**Appendix D   Case Study #3: Eastman Kodak Company—
A Manufacturing Success Story** **81**

Contributing Authors. *85*
Index. *87*

List of Figures and Tables

Chapter 1

Table 1.1	A traditional company versus a lean company........................	2
Figure 1.1	A value stream map...	6
Figure 1.2	Working on value-added activities versus working on non-value-added activities....................................	8
Figure 1.3	Plan–do–check–act cycle.	10
Figure 1.4	Three-sigma and six-sigma processes.....................................	15
Table 1.2	Defect levels corresponding to sigma levels.	15
Table 1.3	Sigma level examples.	16
Table 1.4	Sigma level related to cost of quality.	17
Table 1.5	The DMAIC phases, outputs, and tools....................................	19
Table 1.6	Goals and tools of lean and Six Sigma.	22

Chapter 2

Figure 2.1	Hidden costs of quality and the multiplier effect.....................	36
Figure 2.2	New model of optimum quality costs.	37
Figure 2.3	The P&L statement for the improvements.	40
Figure 2.4	The balance sheet for the improvements.................................	41

Chapter 3

Table 3.1	Examples of key performance indicators...............................	52
Figure 3.1	Dashboard example for a shipping function.	55

Introduction

I f, as is often said, we are what we eat, then it may follow that we are also what we read. If nothing else, books that broaden our knowledge are indeed food for the brain.

That is the purpose of the ASQ Quality Management Division's book series on the Economics of Quality—to stimulate thought on how different quality methods can be used to influence the financial position of an organization.

A manager who wants to know about a popular business topic, an engineer responsible for cost control who needs a good business tool, or a person new to the quality profession who wants to understand more about the many different approaches to drive organizational success—what we all seek is answers to two simple questions, What is it? and How do I get started? This book series has those answers.

The Economics of Quality series is written by subject matter experts from business, academia, consulting, and not-for-profit organizations. They represent the best minds on the subject about which they write.

This series is not intended to be application guides. It is introductory material to point us in the right direction so we know what the capabilities of a method are. These books are intended to arm us with the right questions so that if we want to deploy a particular methodology, we know what to ask in order to move to the next step in the implementation process.

The subject matter experts of the Quality Management Division are members of a variety of Division Technical Committees who have specific and in-depth knowledge about methods such as ISO, lean/Six Sigma, quality costs, employee involvement, quality management information systems, globalization/supply chain, data-driven decision making, and quality in project management.

In addition to sharing their expertise through books like this one, the committees contribute to business journals and speak at quality and business conferences.

You can find out more about the Quality Management Division through the American Society for Quality Web site: www.asq.org. As a member of the greater Society and Quality Management Division you will benefit from the professional contributions of our technical committees and other subject matter experts. The Division publishes a peer reviewed journal, *The Quality Management Forum,* that provides in-depth application guidance to improve all types of organizations. As a member, you will also have the opportunity to attend our annual conference dedicated to quality and organizational improvement. Our goal is to help make all organizations and broader society a better place to work and live.

William H. Denney, PhD
Vice Chair, Technical Committees
Quality Management Division
American Society for Quality
2007

Preface

This work is part of ASQ's Economics of Quality book series, a collection of volumes on non-technology-driven innovation that applies to all markets and organizations. It is intended to provide a fundamental introduction to the concepts of lean enterprise and Six Sigma for executives, personnel new to quality, or organizations interested in introductory information on quality and process improvement. This book is not intended to be used as a handbook or as an in-depth exploration of the underlying methodologies, but rather a helpful guide to implementing and optimizing an integrated "Lean Six Sigma" approach focused on realizing return value and bottom line impact.

The principles of lean and Six Sigma will be introduced and discussed both separately and using an integrated approach across the book's three chapters. Chapter 1 provides an overview of each concept independently, including commonly used tools and terminology. In addition, suggestions are offered to help prepare organizations for implementation. The second chapter begins with a refresher on important financial measures, emphasizing the economic benefits of utilizing Lean Six Sigma to improve profitability. Quality costs are also discussed to help managers develop a sound investment strategy and categorize costs, with a goal of maximizing preventive activities and minimizing failures and waste. Once the fundamental principles have been established, Chapter 3 focuses solely on implementing a Lean Six Sigma–based initiative and shares valuable insight to let managers know what to expect and help them steer clear of organizational roadblocks.

Manufacturing and nonmanufacturing firms who are just starting or contemplating a Lean Six Sigma initiative will find this book especially valuable. To aid in illustrating the application of these principles to diverse and global businesses, various case studies have been selected and included to demonstrate how the prescribed tools and techniques can accommodate and enhance a wide variety of customer relationships throughout the value chain. Examples taken from manufacturing, banking, and local government demonstrate the broad spectrum across which Lean Six Sigma can be used as a framework to foster improved performance and ensure continued customer satisfaction and loyalty.

We hope you find this overview of Lean Six Sigma enjoyable and informative and wish you success on your journey.

R. Meisel
S. Babb
S. Marsh
J. Schlichting

1

Lean, Six Sigma, and Lean Six Sigma

Two approaches to improvement to avoid: systems without passion and passion without systems.

Tom Peters, *Thriving on Chaos,* 1987

BACKGROUND

Lean and Six Sigma are two quality initiatives that have received much attention and publicity in the last decade. They each incorporate a philosophy, a methodology, and a toolkit to help organizations improve their business results. Each has shown documented, quantifiable financial impact on implementing organizations. Used together, there is a synergistic effect that accelerates this impact.

The early concepts of lean actually date back to Henry Ford's use of a mass-production system based on work flow. In Japan these concepts were expanded by the Toyoda family in their spinning and weaving plant and were further developed in the family's Motor Company, evolving into what is known today as the Toyota Production System.

Six Sigma was first developed at Motorola in the 1980s as an initiative to save its troubled pager business. Six Sigma became popular in the 1990s after much publicity was generated around its use at General Electric and AlliedSignal and the successes those two companies were achieving.

Both lean and Six Sigma focus on customer satisfaction and improved business performance. These two methodologies also focus on improving a wide variety of processes—new product development, administration, customer service, finance, manufacturing, supply chain, healthcare, and so on. Both methodologies use project management to drive results.

Combining the principles and tools of these methodologies can accelerate the rate of improvement. Lean Six Sigma uses both of the toolkits. This approach integrates both disciplines—lean (time and waste reduction) and Six Sigma (process variability reduction)—by focusing on value to the customer and on business improvement. In the end, an organization should strive to be a lean enterprise with Six Sigma capability.

LEAN

The goal of lean is to increase speed through the relentless elimination of waste from our processes. Companies that have implemented lean have very different characteristics from traditional companies that have not done so. Some of these characteristics are highlighted in Table 1.1; the characteristics of the lean company demonstrate the benefits of implementation.

The underlying concept of lean is developing eyes for waste. Waste is defined as anything that does not add value from the customer's perspective. The five principles of lean, as defined by Womack and Jones, are as follows:

Value—something defined by the customer and created by the producer that the customer is willing to pay for

Value stream—the set of all actions required to bring products, goods, or services to the customer

Table 1.1   A traditional company versus a lean company.

Traditional company	Lean company
Complex	Simple/visual
Forecast/budget driven	Demand driven
Excess inventory	Inventory as needed
Speed up value-added work	Reduce non-value-added activities
Batch production	Small lot size
Long lead times	Minimal lead time
Quality inspected or sorted in	Quality built and designed in
Functional departments	Value stream managers

Flow—smooth movement through the process

Pull—a technique where the downstream customer triggers the need for the product or service

Perfection—no errors made, no defects generated

Putting these concepts together, an organization accurately specifies value, identifies the entire value stream, makes the value-added steps flow continuously, lets the customers pull value from the organization, and provides defect-free products and services. The idea is to create ever-increasing value for the customer and/or business by improving the value stream, often unblocking flow problems in the process.

Types of Waste

Lean thinking allows an organization to improve its value stream by removing all forms of waste from the system. Lean thinking recognizes seven types of waste: correction, motion, overproduction, conveyance, inventory, processing, and waiting.

Correction. This type of waste is reflected in a company's need to repair or rework product or services because of defects that may be the result of faulty workmanship, incorrect procedures, nonconforming raw materials, lack of information, and so on. And while the category is called correction, it also includes the scrap that results from the creation of defects. In a manufacturing environment, scrap is often easy to see—by just walking around and looking in waste receptacles. Repair and rework are not always as visible but can usually be found. Juran referred to these elements as the *hidden factory*—that portion of a process that typically does not show up on a flowchart. It is the 'standard' part of the operation that exists solely to correct mistakes, errors, and defects, including the retesting of repaired product. An example of correction in an office environment would be creating a faulty report or invoice, printing it out, and finding the errors internally—or worse, sending it to the customer and then finding out about the errors—followed by correcting those errors, then reprinting and resending the document with apologies or some more expensive form of recompense.

Motion. The waste here is any kind of excess motion required in order to complete a task. This could involve production workers lifting heavy containers from the floor to a table or conveyer belt. It could be office workers stretching or bending to get something in their desk. Or it could be walking to another building that houses central supplies in order to get a needed item. All of these examples take workers away from value-added work and sometimes entail a safety or health risk. And while these examples may seem like small, even miniscule, measures of waste, they do add up. If every person in the organization spends as little as five minutes a day on these sorts of "built-in" wasted motions, that adds up to 25 minutes per week, which is more than 20 hours per year per worker.

Overproduction. This is the waste of producing more than is needed. Maybe you make more finished product in manufacturing because there is some additional raw material available or half an hour remaining on the shift. Or you might make different versions of a product because you are not quite sure what the customer will buy or how much. You might make more than you think you need because you fear that some of the product might be defective. Or you make 15 copies of a report for a meeting for which 13 people have acknowledged they will attend, just in case two more people actually show up. Overproduction wastes time and money, preventing both of those resources from being used for something else. And this type of waste can never be recouped.

Conveyance. This is the waste that occurs with *unnecessary* movement of goods such as transporting goods (raw materials, component parts, or finished product) into or out of storage or between processes. It can include trucking material from one city to another or shipping it across the ocean to perform the next step of the operation. It could be the movement of material by forklift truck from one side of a building to another. In an office environment, a person might need to walk up one floor to get output from the central printer or walk to a copy center to duplicate a report.

Inventory. Maintaining excess amounts of raw materials, parts, in-process goods, or finished products is waste. This type of inventory can be the result of overproduction for any of the reasons listed in that section. The excess inventory that is created intentionally to counter known or potential quality issues is called safety stock. And inventory waste is not restricted to manufacturing operations. Many offices park a full pallet of paper next to each copier that will take months to use up; less paper at each copier would occupy less space and would tie up less money.

Processing. Sometime referred to as overprocessing, this means doing more work than is necessary to accomplish a task. In equipment manufacturing, how polished does a part need to be that will be inside the product, not visible to the customer? Do we double-wrap product when a single layer will protect it, or use twice as much twine to tie the package? How many approvals are necessary to order supplies or to make a change? And how many (multiple) times are data entered into various information systems? All of these examples expose potential processing waste.

Waiting. The meaning of this term is just what you think—people being idle because their work cannot proceed. And this can be for a variety of reasons. An operator runs out of raw material and needs to replenish the stock. Or maybe the stock had been replenished but the material delivered was incorrect or defective. When one machine is used to make different products, it may take time to make the changeover from one job to the next. In an office, a purchasing agent may be waiting for approval to order material, or a Human Resource representative has to ask for additional information from a job applicant before processing the application further.

These seven wastes are not necessarily independent. Production of safety stock, by itself, is overproduction. But if it is produced because of defect issues, that overproduction is also tied to the waste of correction and inventory waste. Or consider the example of someone who walks to a central printer to retrieve a document. There is wasted motion in getting up from the chair. And there is conveyance waste in walking from the printer to the office carrying the document. Does walking from the office to the printer constitute motion waste or conveyance waste? While some people would spend time debating the issue (a waste of time in itself), the bottom line is that it doesn't matter! As long as the waste is identified, the key is to find a way to eliminate it.

Value Stream Mapping and Analysis

One of the first steps in getting the waste out of a system is constructing a *value stream map* (VSM). The VSM links the customer through the company's processes and back to the supplier. It does this two ways: it follows the material flow from the supplier through to the customer and at the same time it shows the information flow from the customer back through to the supplier. A VSM extends beyond the concept of supply chain management by including the customer.

Typically, a VSM will include a time scale at the bottom showing the value-added time as well as the overall lead time. There are also data boxes for each step of the process. These boxes contain details on changeover time, uptime, defect levels, and so forth. An example of a VSM is shown in Figure 1.1.

Organizations should start with a current-state value stream map, which shows the path from order to delivery under current conditions. The material and information flow, coupled with the other data, can be used to identify where waste exists, which in turn leads to identifying opportunities for improvement. In general there are four stages in constructing and using a VSM:

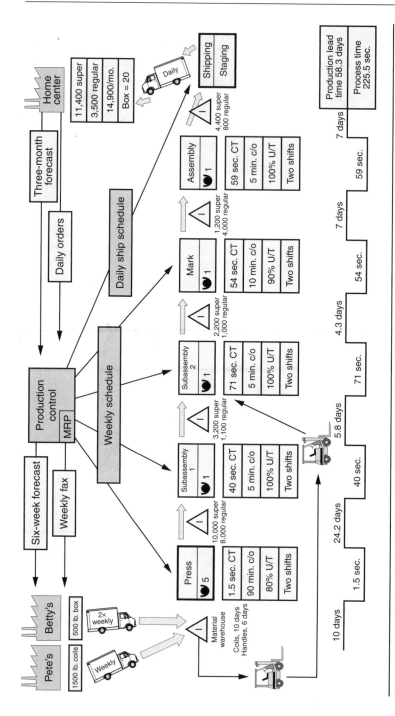

Figure 1.1 A value stream map.
Based on Mike Rother and John Shook, *Learning to See* (Brookline, MA: The Lean Enterprise Institute, 1999): 28–29.

1. Diagram the current flow of the process.

   a. Start with the customer.

   b. Add the process steps.

   c. Show where the raw materials come from and where finished materials go.

   d. Add the information flow, the timeline, and other relevant data.

2. Identify waste by questioning *every* step.

   a. Is the step necessary?

   b. What would happen if the step were removed?

   c. Could the step be part of the previous operation?

3. Draw a future-state VSM that shows what the process will look like when the waste has been removed.

   a. Can the current process be rearranged for efficiency?

   b. Will a different layout reduce transportation and material handling?

4. Develop a work plan to get from the current-state VSM to the future-state VSM.

In essence, the current-state VSM is used to identify opportunities for improvement, that is, areas for waste reduction. With these opportunities in mind, a future-state map can be developed. The future-state map must *not* be limited by what is in the current flow of the process. Instead, developing the future-state VSM allows—indeed requires—that the customer and the customer's needs be made part of the value stream map. For example, how many units are required by customer X per month? What drives the marketing plan? Are customers involved? How accurate is the sales forecast? What is the sales forecast based on?

The total cycle time then needs to be analyzed. We are looking for opportunities to implement change and create savings. The cycle time analysis must include the time required for all major steps, individual tasks, subprocesses, and so on, that are part of the process, from beginning to end, whether they are value-added or not. The analysis then needs to define whether the activity is value-added. One gauge of a process is the percent of total cycle time spent on value-adding activities. A typical percentage for many processes is five to 10 percent. To put this in context, companies who have been working on lean implementation for years have achieved value-added percentages as high as 45 to 50 percent.

Traditional process improvement has focused on the value-added portion of the total cycle time, which is usually a small portion of the overall process and a minor contributor to the total lead time. The realization that value-added steps typically constitute a small percentage of total cycle time was never apparent until the growth and acceptance of lean thinking.

WHY WORK ON NON-VALUE-ADDING STEPS?

Think about it. Let's consider a process with an overall cycle time of 20 hours, and generously assume that 10 percent, that is, two hours, comprises value-added activities. If we work on the value-added steps of the process and achieve a 50 percent improvement, the value-added steps now take one hour and the overall process takes 19 hours. If, on the other hand, we focus on the true areas of waste—the non-value-adding steps—and achieve a 50 percent improvement in those, our non-value-added steps take nine hours and the overall process takes 11 hours. That's a much greater overall reduction than the traditional approach. This is shown graphically in Figure 1.2.

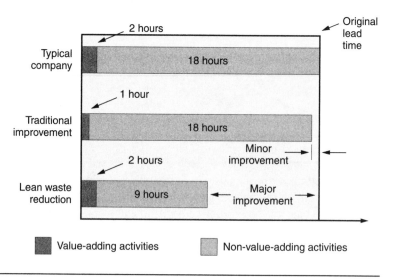

Figure 1.2   Working on value-added activities versus working on non-value-added activities.

Once the activities have been categorized, further analysis can be performed. If an activity is value-added, we can see if there is some way to simplify it and reduce the time spent. If the activity is non-value-added, we might want to classify it as necessary or not. Even if it doesn't change the form, fit, or function of the product, and even if the customer would not want to pay for the activity, we might still need to do it. It might be required for government regulations, such as FDA compliance, or it might be necessary for business success. From a lean perspective, billing is non-value-added, but we still need to do it to stay in business. So, for steps that are non-value-added but necessary, we again look to streamline, simplify, and reduce the amount of time spent. For those non-value-added activities that are not necessary, we work at eliminating them.

Lean Tools That Can Help Make These Improvements

Up to this point we have seen how lean thinking can identify opportunities for improvement. The next logical progression is to consider how these improvements are to be made.

PDCA

One of the core elements of lean methodology is the plan–do–check–act (PDCA) cycle (see Figure 1.3). Carry out improvement activities by following the PDCA process:

Plan

- Scope the activity so that you know where the task at hand starts and stops

- Ensure that this scope is manageable in the time allowed

- Set the improvement targets

- Engage the right people in the activity

- Make all logistical arrangements

- Get any pre-work completed

Do

- Consider the possible approaches

- Try those that seem most feasible

- Focus on those that look most promising

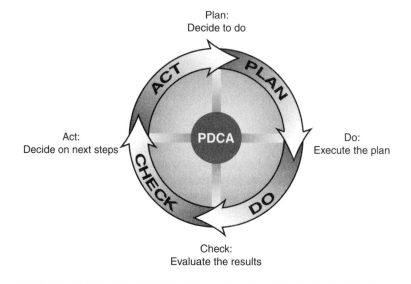

Plan:
Decide to do

Act:
Decide on next steps

Do:
Execute the plan

Check:
Evaluate the results

Figure 1.3   Plan–do–check–act cycle.

Check

• See if you were able to meet your objectives

Act

• If you accomplished what you set out to do, standardize on the new method—standard work is a key component of lean thinking

• If you did not achieve all you set out to do, cycle back to the *plan* stage to see what else needs to be done

Kaizen

Kaizen is a Japanese word (not a proper name) that means "continuous improvement." It is an underlying philosophy of lean thinking. Kaizen is also commonly associated with specific improvement events, sometimes called *kaizen events, kaizen blitzes,* or *kaizen bursts.* These are specific events intended to result in targeted improvements. They are formalized activites using the PDCA method described above. When an organization is in the early stages of implementing lean, these events are often three to five days in length. A team is put in place for the event, with a designated team leader, sometimes including a coleader and/or a facilitator. At the beginning of the event, the problem is clearly defined, and both daily and overall targets for improvement are established. The management sponsor usually kicks off the event, and management reviews are held at the end of each day. This keeps management informed as to progress and engages them in eliminating any barriers that have surfaced during the day. A closing meeting is held with all key stakeholders at the end of the event, followed by team thanks and recognition. As an organization matures in the application of lean, these events become shorter and shorter in duration. The ultimate goal is to have short kaizen bursts, five to 15 minutes in length, occurring throughout the workplace as needed.

5S

Another tool associated with lean thinking is 5S, which is often applied early in the implementation stage of lean and then used as an ongoing method of support. 5S is based on five Japanese terms all starting with the letter S, which have been translated into English terms that also start with S:

Sort. Separate needed from unneeded parts, tools, and supplies, getting rid of what is unneeded

Set in order. Neatly arrange and identify parts for ease of use

Shine. Conduct a clean-up campaign

Standardize. Conduct the first three S's at regular and frequent intervals

Sustain. Form habits to integrate 5S into your processes, and audit to ensure compliance

5S is not just "nice to do." It is a tool that drives an important result: the development and maintenance of an efficient and safe work environment, one of the goals of lean thinking and application.

5S is not solely for a manufacturing environment. Consider your office. Do you have things that you don't really need? Do you know where everything is? Are the things you use most often close at hand? One organization that provides training conducted a 5S activity in their classroom. Items no longer being used were discarded, things were rearranged so that items used by instructors were in nearby cabinets at the front of the room, storage shelves were labeled so that items could be easily found and returned to the correct location. In today's information age, think about your computer files. How much time do you spend looking for a file that you want? Do you have files on your disk drive that you no longer need?

5S IN YOUR GARAGE

Think of what would be involved in performing 5S on your garage or basement. You would first look at everything that is there and decide what you need and what you don't (*sort*). Then comes the hard part for some people—get rid of what you don't absolutely need. Once you have only what you need, *set in order*. Decide where things should go, considering what items you use most often and where you use them. Label them—use tags to indicate where they go, or draw an outline around them on the wall. Then spruce up the area (*shine*), making sure everything is clean and in good working order. *Standardize* means that you will put things back in the right place, you will periodically examine what you have to make sure you need everything, and you will perform routine cleaning. Then you need to *sustain* by making sure that all of the above takes place on an ongoing basis, possibly using periodic audits.

Are the files arranged for easy access? How frequently do you purge obsolete files? How much more efficient would you be if 5S were performed on your computer files?

Other Lean Tools

Other lean tools and concepts that also merit mention include:

Visual management. Having good simple measures that are visible to all so that anybody (particularly management) walking through the area can tell at a glance how things are going—whether you are ahead of or behind schedule, quality performance, safety performance, and so on

Just in time. Providing the right amount of the right product/ service that the customer wants at just the time the customer wants it; no more, no less, no sooner, no later

Jidoka. Individual control of the operation so the workers can stop the process when a problem occurs, call for needed assistance, and wait for correction before resuming work

Standard work. A well-defined set of procedures performed in a prescribed manner at a pace dictated by customer usage

One-piece flow. Less inventory is accumulated and less waiting occurs when items are produced one at a time, flowing through the process at the pace of customer pull

SIX SIGMA

The goal of Six Sigma is to reduce costs and increase profits by eliminating variability, defects, and waste, all of which ultimately undermine customer satisfaction and loyalty. Variation—the spread of data around the average value—can be a key cause of defective goods and services. The statistical description of variation is called the *standard deviation,* which is symbolized by the Greek letter sigma (σ).

Jack Welch, the chief driver of Six Sigma at General Electric, made the following observation about variation:

> We have been working on moving the mean. The problem is the mean never happens. The customer only feels the variance that we have not yet removed. Variation is evil in any customer-touching process. Improvement to our internal processes is of no interest to the customer. (Jack Welch and Suzy Welch, *Winning* [New York: HarperCollins, 2005]: 251.)

In the past, improvement efforts were often focused on getting processes to operate at the correct level, that is, the mean. Welch clearly points out the inherent fallacy of that idea—the average is a calculated value, not a value that actually occurs. What good is an average delivery time of six days if some customers experience delivery in four days (and possibly need to scramble for storage space) while others wait eight days for their merchandise? He goes on to say that "Once you understand the simple maxim 'variation is evil,' you're 60 percent of the way to becoming a Six Sigma expert yourself. The other 40 percent is getting the evil out." And this is the basis for Six Sigma—getting that evil variation out of the system.

Six Sigma can be viewed in three different ways: as a philosophy, as a metric, and as a methodology.

The Six Sigma Philosophy

To reduce variation in all the aspects of the business and make customer-focused, data-driven decisions is the Six Sigma philosophy. Six Sigma starts with the premise that all work is a process and that all processes have variability. We need to eliminate harmful, event-driven sources of variation while also reducing the noise in the system. In order to do this, we need hard data, not a "gut feel" or sense of "what might fix it." The data we need has to be meaningful and must also be related either directly or ultimately to customer needs or expectations. Philosophically, the goal of Six Sigma is to achieve zero defects through data-based variation reduction. And in Six Sigma, defects are not just flaws in a manufactured product. They are defined much more broadly as "any nonconformity or error in processes or products." If it were possible to eliminate all variability, not only would defects disappear but performance would improve as well. All of which would lead to quality excellence in products or services and vast improvement in profits. Another benefit that is often overlooked is the dramatic improvement in employee morale that occurs when processes are smoothed—that is, when variability is reduced.

The Six Sigma Metric

This is defined as 3.4 defects per million opportunities (DPMO). Let's not get hung up on the term "opportunities." This is a counting mechanism used in Six Sigma to account for the differing complexity of processes, allowing comparison on an apples-to-apples basis. The essence of the measure is that 3.4 defects per million opportunities represents a very good level of quality, that is, a very low level of defects. The measure of 3.4 DPMO is not one that was selected just because it sounds good. In fact, it's a number that is based on very sound statistical theory.

Let's start with the idea that many processes can be described by a bell-shaped, symmetrical curve called the normal distribution. In addition we will assume we have valid specification limits, that is, requirements that are driven by customer needs and expectations. When we superimpose the process distribution onto the specification limits for a "typical" process (one operating at an "average" quality level), we see that the specifications cross the process distribution at plus and minus three standard deviations. Thus this would be designated a three-sigma process. If we work on reducing the variation in that process, the shape of the distribution narrows as the standard deviation decreases. If we reduce the variation so that the standard deviation is half as big as it was, the specifications will cross the process distribution at plus and minus six standard deviations. This process will then be described as operating at a six sigma level of quality. This is shown in Figure 1.4.

With a normal distribution, statistical calculations can be used to determine the amount of the process distribution that will fall outside of the specification limits. For the three-sigma process shown in Figure 1.4, 0.27 percent of the area under the curve is outside of the specifications, a defect level of 2700 DPMO. For the six-sigma process, that level is about 0.002

DPMO, or two defects per billion opportunities. When Six Sigma methodology was developed, there was recognition that processes may shift from
their nominal or target value. Defect levels were calculated assuming that
the mean shifts by 1.5 standard deviations, so the defect levels associated
with three-sigma and six-sigma processes are 66,811 DPMO and 3.4 DPMO,
respectively. Table 1.2 shows the defect levels for other sigma levels.

As you know already, corrective action needs to be taken any time a
process deviates from its target value. In the case of a three-sigma process

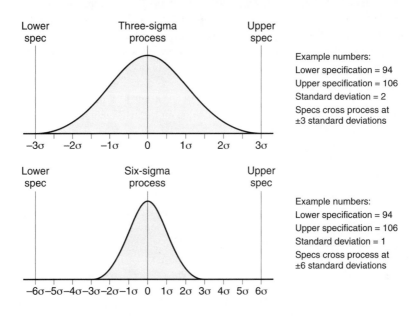

Figure 1.4   Three-sigma and six-sigma processes.

Table 1.2   Defect levels corresponding
to sigma levels.

Sigma level	DPMO
2	308,770
3	66,811
4	6,210
5	233
6	3.4

(the upper curve in Figure 1.4), deviation from the aim—that is, a shift in the process distribution to the left or the right—significantly increases the amount of material outside the specification limits. If the process is operating at a six-sigma level of quality, there is very little nonconforming product produced by a process shift. You still need to correct the process, even at a six-sigma level of performance, but neither the customer nor the internal process will be as significantly affected.

You might be wondering why quality needs to be this good. While arguments like "more discriminating customers" and "tougher competition" support the need for six-sigma quality levels, Table 1.3 makes some startling comparisons to underscore those arguments.

The sigma level of a process thus becomes a metric related to quality. While six sigma is not the same as zero defects, it is a significant threshold of performance. Many companies get started on the path to six sigma when they are operating at only a three-sigma level of performance and they know they have to make significant, even radical, changes to drive to a six-sigma level of performance.

Sigma levels can also be related to another measure: the cost of quality (COQ). While COQ will be addressed in more detail in Chapter 2, let's take a brief high-level look at it. For a typical company operating at a three-sigma level, the cost of quality can be as much as 25 to 40 percent of its sales. These costs include supplier qualification, product testing, scrap, rework, and customer returns, just to name a few. While that figure may seem unbelievably high, a multitude of COQ studies can be found to support it. Table 1.4 shows what happens to the cost of quality as the sigma level increases.

Table 1.3   Sigma level examples.

Three-sigma quality level	Six-sigma quality level
54,000 incorrect drug prescriptions per year	Three incorrect drug prescriptions every year
40,500 newborn babies dropped each year	Two newborn babies dropped each year
No electricity, water, or heat for two hours a month	No electricity, water, or heat for one second every two years
Five long or short landings at O'Hare Airport each day	One long or short landing at O'Hare Airport every 10 years
5400 lost articles of mail per hour	65 lost articles of mail per day

Table 1.4   Sigma level related to cost of quality.

Sigma level	DPMO	Cost of quality (COQ)
2	308,770	> 40 percent of sales
3	66,807	25 to 40 percent of sales
4	6,210	15 to 25 percent of sales
5	233	5 to 15 percent of sales
6	3.4	< 5 percent of sales

The Six Sigma Methodology

Six Sigma uses a problem-solving process (based on the plan–do–check–act cycle) known as DMAIC: define, measure, analyze, improve, and control. All Six Sigma improvement projects follow these steps. Let's take a look at each of the phases of the DMAIC process.

Define. Management charters the project and typically provides some expectations and specific deliverables. At this stage, the project's purpose, scope, and scale are defined and resources are allocated so that a team is formed. Initial information is collected on the process and customer needs to define the problem.

Measure. The team creates a baseline to determine current performance of the process. This is important not only as a starting point but it is also important later in the Six Sigma process to gauge the overall effect of the improvements made. The team might also find it necessary to conduct a measurement systems analysis (MSA) to see whether the current system is adequate for the intended use.

Analyze. The team then identifies possible sources of the variation, investigates what underlies those sources (root cause), and conducts experiments to test and verify the true cause of the variation. The classic sources of variation are man (people), machine (equipment), methods (procedures), materials, measurement, and environment (overall operating conditions). Various methods are used to determine the root cause, such as the five whys. The typical statistical tools used to verify root causes include design of experiments (DOE) and hypothesis testing. A crucial aspect in successfully analyzing the root cause of an issue is to include the key personnel associated with the process. These people will likely be the operators, engineers, process experts, and so forth.

Improve. Lasting process improvements or countermeasures to address the root cause are determined. The optimum improvement should be selected on the basis of probability of success, time to execute, impact on resources, and cost to implement. A small-scale implementation should be conducted and evaluated prior to proceeding to the full-scale implementation.

Control. Means of evaluating the implemented solutions and maintaining the gains need to be put in place at this point. Once the full-scale implementation has been verified, standardizing the process and installing early-warning detection methods to identify when a process is trending out of control are the appropriate steps. Remember that the goals are to control the inputs and monitor the outputs, thus reducing variation. This phase includes monitoring over time to ensure that improvement has been made and savings are being realized.

The phases, their outputs, and the tools used in each are summarized in Table 1.5. Keep in mind that the list of tools is meant to be representative only. They are the tools most commonly used but the list is by no means exhaustive. Nor do you have to use all of the tools in each phase. The project itself will dictate the most appropriate tools to use.

Six Sigma takes place on a project-by-project basis. Success of the initiative is dependent on many key stakeholders—management/executive sponsors, champions, process owners, Belts, team members, and financial analysts. Their roles and responsibilities are described below.

Management/Executive Sponsors. These are the upper-level people who are creating and driving the Six Sigma effort for the organization. They create strategic plans and business plans and they work on strategic policy deployment. This includes developing a list of potential projects, prioritizing that list, and deciding which projects need to be implemented and when. They provide the resources for training and consulting and establish project-tracking and management systems. Ultimately it is their responsibility to create a conducive environment for Six Sigma.

Champions. These people are often responsible for the successful implementation of Six Sigma in an organization or a department. They understand the Six Sigma methodology and serve as the link to the leadership team. The Champions select projects for each department, monitor their execution, and ensure that the gains are realized. Champions make sure that the projects being implemented are tied to the organization's strategic plan. They also help drive cross-functional coordination of projects and help match the Belts to given projects. Champions communicate the teams' successes throughout the organization and are responsible for reward and recognition of the teams.

Table 1.5 The DMAIC phases, outputs, and tools.

Phase	Outputs	Tools

Define	• Project charter
	  – Problem statement
	  – Project scope, scale, and boundaries
	  – Project team
	  – Gantt chart/timeline
	  – Improvement goals and objectives
	• Process map
	• SIPOC model
	• Voice of the customer
		• Project management tools
		• Flowcharting
		• SIPOC (supplier–input–process–output–customer) analysis
		• Pareto analysis
		• Voice of the customer studies
		• Kano model
		• Quality function deployment (QFD)
		• Affinity diagrams

Measure	• Baseline data • Process capability • Measurement systems analysis (MSA) or gage R&R • Refined project charter and/or problem statement • Refined process map	• Data gathering plan • Check sheets/spreadsheets • Descriptive statistics • Pareto chart • Control charts • Measurement systems analysis • Failure mode and effects analysis (FMEA)
Analyze	• Identified root cause(s) • Validated root cause(s)	• Brainstorming • Cause-and-effect diagrams • Control charts • Scatter plots • Root cause analysis • Pareto analysis • FMEA • Inferential statistics (hypothesis testing) • Design of experiments (DOE)
Improve	• Prioritized improvements/countermeasures • Improvement plan • Validated solutions or improvements	• Data collection • FMEA • Hypothesis testing • Design of experiments • Simulation • Mistake-proofing and failsafing • Cost analysis

Continued

Continued

Phase	Outputs	Tools
Control	• Quantification of the improvements • Standard operating procedures (SOPs) • Control plan • Documentation of the project	• Control charts • Process map • Standardization • Mistake-proofing and failsafing • Process dashboards and scorecards • Cost of quality • Overall cost analysis

Use only the tools necessary; not all tools are required.

Process Owners. These people are responsible for the process that is going to be improved by the project. They must be involved in the original definition of the project. They should also help identify key resources including who should be part of the project team and with whom the team needs to work. Process owners help schedule times when the process can be disrupted in support of the improvement efforts and they usually have line responsibility for the process being improved. These individuals can be (but don't have to be) the direct supervisor of the Black or Green Belt leading the project.

Master Black Belts. These are experts on Six Sigma tools and concepts. Some organizations develop and/or hire their own Master Black Belts; other organizations contract these resources. While their roles vary somewhat from company to company, Master Black Belts usually conduct Six Sigma training for the organization. This always includes Black Belt training and could include Green Belt training. The Master Black Belts coach and mentor the Belt candidates to ensure proper application of methods and tools. They often lead or support high-level projects, which could be cross-functional in nature. They also assist Champions and process owners with project selection and project management.

Black Belts (BB). These are change agents who are trained in Six Sigma processes and tools and as a result lead and facilitate project teams. At many companies the Black Belt role is a full-time position for a designated period of time, often two years. At other companies they are not full-time, but are embedded in the organization with Black Belt responsibilities as part of their duties. Black Belts usually come from line positions and go through four or five weeks of training on Six Sigma. They are certified as Black Belts by completing the training and the required number of Six Sigma projects; some companies require one project, others require two. Black Belts are dedicated Six Sigma practitioners, highly trained Six Sigma project leaders, and experts in DMAIC. In addition to leading projects, they also mentor other people. When their assignment as a Black Belt is completed, they reenter the organization in a line position where they continue to apply their skills.

Green Belts (GB). These people are also change agents and have a similar role to that of Black Belts. The role of the Green Belts differs from company to company. In some organizations, Green Belts receive the same training as Black Belts but their role is part-time and their projects can be narrower in scope. In other organizations the Green Belts receive less training, so that their tool kit is not quite as extensive. Green Belts also act as team members for Black Belt projects.

Team Members. While Black Belts or Green Belts typically lead or facilitate Six Sigma projects, the project team consists of other individuals known as team members. Team members can be viewed as subject matter experts who bring necessary skills and knowledge to the project. They usually contribute their skills to the project on a part-time basis. They are trained in specific aspects necessary for project success but typically they do not receive complete Six Sigma training.

Financial Analysts. People from Finance have been involved in Six Sigma efforts at most companies that report successful implementation. These people help develop potential savings estimates during the *define* phase, assist in documenting project results at various stages of the project, and monitor success 12 months after the project is completed.

LEAN VERSUS SIX SIGMA OR LEAN AND SIX SIGMA?

Up to now, we have dealt with lean and Six Sigma as two separate, independent efforts. They arose from different industries and needs, they seem to address different issues, they have different implementation approaches, and they have different sets of tools. And in some companies the programs appear to be at odds with each other. A summary of the goals and some tools of each is shown in Table 1.6.

But the use of lean and Six Sigma tools does not need to be an either/or proposition. Lean tools are generally used to address flow issues while Six Sigma tools are generally used to address variation issues. However, these

Table 1.6   Goals and tools of lean and Six Sigma.

	Lean	**Six Sigma**
Goals	• One-piece flow • Just-in-time inventory • Visual factory • Agile manufacturing • Higher value-added percentage • Overall equipment effectiveness • Work flow standardization	• Defect prevention • 3.4 defects per million • Reducing variation • Stability • Predictable processes • Solve complex problems • Improve value stream
Tools	• Cellular design • Value stream mapping • 5S workplace organization • Kanban and pull system • Setup reduction (SMED) • Total productive maintenance • Poka-yoke • Kaizen blitz	• DMAIC • Statistical tools • Voice of the customer • SIPOC • FMEA • Process mapping • Measurement systems analysis • Design of experiments

are not mutually exclusive. Flow is negatively affected by excessive variation and rework; quality is negatively affected by unnecessary complexity in a process. The ability to go back and forth between the two methodologies, in a Lean Six Sigma culture, is a real plus and results in accelerated improvement.

Ideally, lean and Six Sigma philosophies, methods, and processes are combined in a synergistic way to become known as Lean Six Sigma (or Lean Sigma). Training combines the tools into one toolkit. As a project progresses from inception to completion, the appropriate tool is used regardless of whether it comes from traditional Six Sigma methods or traditional lean methods. The origin should be transparent. The important thing is to use the right tool at the right time to accomplish the objective. A manufacturing or business process may be overly complex and convoluted; streamlining may be required before variation can be characterized and subsequently reduced. Conversely, excess variation may be masking what is really happening in a process. The variation needs to be reduced before other work can be done and before standardization can be instituted. By eliminating waste, the speed of responding to customer needs is increased; by eliminating variation, quality and value for the customer is created. Therefore both technologies, when used together, produce a higher-quality product at a faster pace, which is what customers want.

PREPARING FOR LEAN SIX SIGMA

There are many critical success factors required for successful implementation of Lean Six Sigma. These same factors are required for using lean or Six Sigma as stand-alone programs, too.

The first and foremost of these factors is the need for executive-level engagement. Senior management must be visibly in charge, consistently supportive, and willing to play an active role in communication and reward. Lean Six Sigma must be seen as a cultural shift, not the latest program-of-the-month. Senior management must assure linkage of Lean Six Sigma to corporate strategies by utilizing effective goal deployment and performance-tracking methods. They must provide clear prioritization relative to other initiatives, programs, and priorities.

Senior management must learn different methods for making decisions from those they have used in the past. Simply put, all levels of decision making must use facts and data to support actions. They must understand and rely on statistics for interpreting and clarifying data. And one of the outcomes of committing to fact- and data-based decision making is that management and the organization will need to develop a tolerance for challenging sacred company beliefs. The traditional organizational view needs to be replaced with an external focus on customers and their perspectives. Senior management must establish accountability and define expectations, roles, and responsibilities for the organization. Senior management will be responsible for conducting and participating in regularly scheduled reviews to assure and verify progress of the Lean Six Sigma projects.

Another critical success factor is communication. There must be regular written communications on Lean Six Sigma news and successes. Communication aids are developed and disseminated by and for management. A common language is created and advocated based on Lean Six Sigma. Lean Six Sigma is visibly promoted in every company meeting and communication. Another element of successful programs that is easily overlooked is the need for creating and communicating a human resources plan to support the various roles for Lean Six Sigma.

The next critical success factor is the project itself. A project pipeline spanning at least one year must be created and continually refreshed. The project must be linked to critical business and customer needs. The project's scope and size must be defined in such a way as to produce significant savings and still be achievable. A Champion and Black Belt must be assigned to each project and held accountable. Other key resources also need to be assigned. It has also been found helpful to implement a project-tracking system that will help keep projects on track by making their progress (or lack thereof) visible. The tracking system can also be used to communicate project results so that the knowledge gained from one project can be applied in other areas.

Another critical success factor for Lean Six Sigma is the need for core knowledge and abilities in a variety of areas, including:

- *Knowledge of systems and value streams.* How interdependent components work toward a common aim. The goal is to optimize value-added components while reducing variation so that customers always get what they want.

- *Knowledge of various tools.* Statistics, data analysis, quality methods, root cause analysis, lean tools, and so on. Teams need to be able to distinguish signal from noise, define true root causes, propose countermeasures, develop improvement plans, and drive the project to completion following structured methods.

- *Knowledge of psychology.* The interpersonal and management skills to sell ideas, motivate teams, make data-based decisions, deal with conflict, and build trust.

Is Lean Six Sigma a Requirement to Doing Business?

No. You probably know many more companies that are operating without it than are using this approach. But think about what you've just read and ask yourself the following questions:

- Do you understand the competitive environment and believe you are ahead of the curve?

- Do your customers willingly accept price increases?

- Does your company have a monopoly in the business?

- Is there no substitute for the product?

- Are you meeting or exceeding your margin targets?

- Is there no market pressure from competitors?

- Are the suppliers at the mercy of your company?

- Is there no way for another company to enter the market with an equivalent, or better, product?

If the answer is yes for any or all of these questions, then your company is in an enviable position. More likely, however, you are experiencing market pressure from all sides. To stay in business, most companies need to reduce costs and improve profit margin. Lean Six Sigma can help. As W. Edwards Deming said, "It is not necessary to change. Success is not mandatory."

Is Lean Six Sigma a Fad or Is It Here to Stay?

There have been various quality approaches before Six Sigma, lean, and Lean Six Sigma: statistical process control (SPC), kaizen, total quality management (TQM), and zero defects, just to name a few. Lean Six Sigma uses aspects of many of its predecessors and packages them in a way that makes for a logical, practical, and successful approach.

Large manufacturing companies have used Lean Six Sigma activities to create major achievements and improvements. This methodology is being adopted by small companies, used in transactional (that is, business and business support) processes such as HR and purchasing, and becoming prevalent in service industry sectors. Small companies have been able to measure financial success, even if that success is on a smaller scale than what large companies have reported. Of course, the investment required of small companies is also smaller.

As long as senior management remains committed to business process improvement with its associated financial impact, *and* as long as Lean Six Sigma continues to deliver those improvements, we believe that Lean Six Sigma is here to stay.

CONCLUSION

Lean, Six Sigma, and Lean Six Sigma initiatives have contributed significant financial benefit to organizations. Is there an investment necessary to apply them? Absolutely! There is training involved, starting at the top. A culture of improvement needs to be established in addition to having knowledgeable resources with which to apply the methods and tools. But does the payback exceed the investment? Absolutely! Kaizen events and Six Sigma projects using these methods have been documented in most companies. The value of these projects, often validated by finance experts, ranges from $10,000 for a single project up to millions of dollars for larger initiatives. In today's competitive economic environment, contributions like these cannot be overlooked.

2

The Dollars and Sense of Improvement

*Quality is free. It's not a gift, but it's free. What costs
money are the unquality things—all the actions that
involve not doing jobs right the first time.*

Philip Crosby, *Quality Is Free,* 1980

T he concept of expressing project improvement results in financial
terms is not new; Juran referred to the language of engineers and
the language of managers when talking about accomplishments. The
language of managers is, of course, dollars. The novelty with Six Sigma,
lean, and Lean Six Sigma is that people are actually applying that concept to their efforts. From its inception, Six Sigma has advocated expressing results in terms of money. All successful Six Sigma efforts have stated
results in terms of money and communicated those results widely within
the company. Companies are quoting Six Sigma benefits in the millions
and billions of dollars. At many companies, members of Finance validate
these results. Lean has followed suit by frequently stating results of kaizen
events and other activities in terms of money. The broadcasting of these
results has generated enthusiasm to continue and expand these efforts.

This chapter deals with techniques for assigning dollar values to
improvement results. We will talk about hard dollars and soft dollars, including factors that are sometimes considered intangible. Benchmarking studies
have shown that not all companies assign these dollar values in exactly the
same way. So there is no one best way to do this. Instead, the key is to be

consistent from department to department within a company without creating another level of bureaucracy to estimate or track project values.

There are many ways to measure business performance. Here is a list, certainly far from exhaustive, showing measures used by some organizations:

- Market share

- Productivity

- Customer satisfaction

- Percent margin/operating profit

- Service quality

- Business growth

- Product reliability

- Defects and scrap

- Time to market

- Order-to-cash cycle time

- Delivery time

- Inventory levels

Improvement efforts may be aimed at increasing the first seven of these, or reducing the last five. Operational measures are often tied to these business measures.

A key factor that distinguishes Six Sigma and lean from previous quality-related efforts is the attention these newer methods receive from top management. One of the primary reasons for this is the link to business results. And perhaps even more visible from management's perspective is the conversion of the improvement results to dollar values. Companies use many different financial measures related to dollars. These include:

- Revenue

- Earnings per share (EPS)

- Profit/earnings ratio (P/E)

- Return on assets (ROA)

- Return on net assets (RONA)

- Economic value added (EVA)

- Return on investment (ROI)

- Earnings before interest, taxes, depreciation, and amortization (EBITDA)

A PRIMER ON FINANCE

Regardless of which of the above financial measures an organization chooses to use, there are three fundamental ways to summarize finances: profit and loss (P&L) statement, balance sheet, and cash flow statement. The basic concepts of these are described in the sections below, with apologies to those who work with these summaries on an everyday basis.

The P&L Statement

This document shows a company's income for a defined period of time. It shows how much money an organization brought in (revenue), how much it spent (expenses and costs), and the difference between the two (= net income). The statement is read from top to bottom. The top line shows the revenues generated. Each line after that deducts various expenses and costs from that revenue until you get to the bottom line, the net income.

Revenue received by a company is a fairly straightforward measure—how much money was taken in for the goods and services provided by the company. A company may sell products to consumers either directly or through channels. The "company" may be a retail store selling products to customers coming to the store or it may sell directly to customers over the Internet. Many manufacturing companies who sell to consumers do so through retail outlets, dealerships, or other partners. In some cases the sale may be a business-to-business sale. Regardless of which method is used, the sum of all money received for the products and services provided to business or end-user customers constitutes the revenue received for that period of time.

There are costs that a company or organization incurs to manufacture and/or provide goods and services to customers. One category of these is direct manufacturing costs, sometimes referred to as the cost of goods sold (COGS). This category includes such things as the cost of raw materials purchased from suppliers, direct labor costs for the people manufacturing the products (along with associated benefit and overhead charges), and depreciation.

When you subtract the COGS for a time period from the revenue for the same time period, you get the gross margin, that is, how much money you made before adjusting for other expenses. This is sometimes called gross profit. Gross margin is one financial measure of performance. We certainly want it to be positive and ideally growing. We can look at gross margin either as an absolute amount or as a percentage of revenue.

There are other expenses that need to be quantified, sometimes categorized as operating expenses. These include research and development (R&D) or engineering expenses and an expense category known as selling, general, and administrative (SG&A) expenses. Some of the elements in SG&A are:

- Sales and marketing

- Finance

- Human resources

- Administration

- Supply chain (transportation, distribution, warehousing, and so on)

- Customer service

There is also a category of expenses for nonrecurring charges. These operating expenses are totaled and then subtracted from the gross margin. The result is known as operating income.

The last expense that is considered is the income tax expense. This is subtracted from the operating income to produce the earnings after income tax, or the net income. The net income number is referred to as the bottom line, another financial measure of performance.

The Balance Sheet

This report shows an organization's assets, liabilities, and equity. Assets are listed on one side of a two-column sheet and liabilities and equity are listed on the other. The two sides need to balance, hence the name of the sheet. Assets are often divided into current and long-term and include things like cash, accounts receivable, inventory (raw material, work in progress, and finished goods), and capital. Liabilities are those financial obligations that a company owes to outside organizations and include accounts payable (invoices and bills), taxes, and short-term debt. Equity is the residual value of a business, calculated as total assets minus total liabilities. Equity includes common and preferred stock, treasury stock, and retained earnings. The balance sheet shows the value of a business improving or declining over time.

The Cash Flow Statement

This indicates how cash flowed into the organization over a specific period of time and how that cash was used. There are three general areas of cash flow: (1) the cash flow from day-to-day business operations, exclusive of investing and financing, also known as the operating cash flow, (2) cash flow from investments, showing the outlay for capital expenditures and acquisitions for the year and indicating cash inflows from the sale of property, equipment, or portions of the business, (3) cash flow from financing, which shows cash received from borrowing and cash used to repay loans.

HOW IMPROVEMENT CONTRIBUTES TO FINANCIALS

Given the financial reports and measures that have been described, Six Sigma and lean initiatives can contribute to either the P&L statement or the balance sheet. In a very simplified view, the P&L statement has two buckets: revenue and costs. Improvement efforts can help either of these, with the intention being to increase revenue and decrease costs. Similar efforts can have a positive impact on the balance sheet by increasing cash or decreasing inventory levels and their associated costs.

There are other ways that savings from improvement efforts are classified. One common method is hard savings and soft savings. Hard savings typically have direct impact on the bottom line or top line of the P&L statement. Bottom-line savings can be found by looking at current costs and finding ways to reduce them. Upward changes in revenue dollars, thus increasing the top line, can be seen in projects that affect the amount of product sold. Examples include reduction in operation or production costs, reduction in transaction costs, reduced head count, and increased throughput (resulting in increased sales or revenue).

Soft savings are often more difficult to quantify and see. One view is that they are assets that are freed up so they can be used for another purpose. They can result in cash flow improvement as well as cost and capital spending avoidance. Soft savings might involve the reduction of cash tied up in inventory or decreased spending of capital. They might be realized through avoidance of a planned capacity enhancement or the elimination of a budgeted staff increase. Soft savings can also include what some people consider intangible improvements: increased customer satisfaction, increased employee satisfaction, and increased safety in the workplace. This group of improvements can be expressed in dollar terms, but the conversion is often less concrete than that for other improvements and may depend more on assumptions.

While hard savings are generally related to the P&L statement and soft savings are linked to the balance sheet, both of them can link to cash flow. Cash flow indicates how effectively the business is managing to juggle income and expenses, and its ability to meet its current expenses. There are several types of projects that can improve cash flow: those that result in cost cutting, an increase in inventory turns (that is, buying less inventory and selling it faster), collecting money faster, or taking advantage of terms from vendors (paying bills later rather than sooner).

Linking process improvements to hard savings and soft savings is one way to categorize financial benefits. Lists of possible improvements can be made for each of the categories, and then guidelines developed to convert the improvements into dollars.

ECONOMICS OF THE SEVEN WASTES

There are other ways to generate lists of potential improvements and their corresponding financial impact. One of them is to look at the seven forms of waste associated with lean thinking. Obviously, the magnitude of each of these will be dependent on the specific company and processes involved; this list is meant to give an idea of what should be considered.

Conveyance

Consider all the ways the product moves, both within the company and in delivery to the customer. Conveyance involves the movement of product within the company, whether it is within one building or from building to building. The former might involve the use of fork trucks and people, while the latter might require a truck or car (and of course a driver). Both of these involve costs that show up as operating expense (the people) and possibly capital (the truck or car), with associated depreciation expenses. Lean and Six Sigma projects could result in reduction or elimination of the movement; this could result in decreased labor costs for the driver or decreased cost of capital if a truck or car could be sold. Conveyance also includes shipment of product from the plant to distribution centers or warehouses, or possibly to the customer. Projects could optimize the quantity of product/material shipped per load, improve the shipping routes, change the mode of shipping to a less expensive way, eliminate the need for overnight shipping, and so forth. All of these result in a direct decrease in operating expenses involved with shipping.

Inventory

Inventory includes the raw materials, work in progress, and finished goods being held by a company. There can be many reasons (justified or not) for having inventory. These include:

- Fluctuation in customer demand

- Uncertainty in customer demand (quantity and product type)

- Long lead times

- Poor quality (necessitating the need for safety stock to meet customer orders)

Inventory requires space, which may be on company premises or rented from someone else. The rental space has a defined expense that shows up on the P&L statement. Space on company premises also has costs associated with it. The inventory also ties up money, either in raw material being held by the company or finished goods that have not yet generated revenue. This has a direct impact on cash flow. The impact of decreasing inventory can be stated financially in a variety of ways. One is to look at balance sheet impact and state the full value. Another is to apply a factor to the inventory dollars and classify the savings as decreased carrying costs. Some companies use a 30 percent factor to quantify this. Alternatively, a cost-of-capital figure can be used as a multiplier of the inventory reduction, with this figure currently often accepted as 13 percent. A practical way to track inventory, which is related to the cost of inventory, is the number of inventory "turns," or full replenishments over a time period. As inventory turns are increased, the cost of inventory is reduced.

Motion

Motion is usually concerned with the movement of people. The raw material depot may be located far away from the production machine or people may need to lift heavy containers of material onto a table or loading station. These are just two examples of wasted motion that can result in loss of productivity, safety incidents, or decreased employee satisfaction. Loss of productivity and accidents can be expressed in dollars fairly easily. A lost-time accident has direct medical costs, costs for the time to complete paperwork, and labor costs for follow-up action, as well as lost productivity costs. There can also be intangible effects such as lower employee morale and negative publicity.

Waiting

Waiting can result from unnecessary transportation and motion but also has other causes. Manufacturing can be waiting for raw materials because the wrong material was brought to the line or the material was defective. They might be waiting for the lab to test the first pieces fabricated before full production takes place. They might be waiting for the maintenance crew to complete a repair. In all of these cases, the waiting amounts to loss of productivity, which in turn translates into dollars. It is true that at times the waiting period can be filled with value-adding work that will be needed at another time. But more often than not, the waiting does reduce productivity.

Overproduction

The general definition of this form of waste is making more than is needed. There are a variety of reasons for this, some of which are linked to inventory issues. Not knowing exactly what the customer wants can lead to making more of each variety of product. A desire to utilize the remaining time on a shift (beyond the known demand) or to finish a batch of raw material can also result in overproduction. Sometimes overproduction is tied to poor quality; if yield is known to be 80 percent, extra goods are made so that 100 percent of customer orders can be completed (assuming good product can be identified through inspection). Reducing the amount of overproduction has direct impact on expenses. Fewer raw materials are used, along with less machine time. If the extra goods typically are stored, reduction in overproduction will be associated with reduced inventory and its corresponding financial impact.

Processing

This should be called "overprocessing" as it describes waste that results from doing more than necessary to complete a task or job. For example, why are three signatures needed to start a job, when in reality it might be started with just one, or even none? A test procedure might call for three samples to be measured because of the high degree of measurement uncertainty. Once the measurement process is improved, can the procedure require fewer samples? Or, how often does your data have to be entered two or three times because computer systems do not communicate with one another? These examples are linked, directly or indirectly, to inventory, waiting, and loss of productivity.

Correction

Correction is required whenever product does not meet requirements, forms are missing information, or product is shipped early or late. Correcting defects means first taking time and resources to recognize bad product. This means incurring the cost of sorting or separating it out—and don't forget the cost of disposing of it! Rework is the most obvious type of correction but there is also the cost of retesting the repaired or reworked product. All of these steps have a direct impact on operating expenses, both in material and labor. If corrections have to be made after the products get into the customer's hands, the costs of making these corrections can rise exponentially and affect warranty costs and goodwill costs, as well as softer costs like decreased customer satisfaction.

COST OF (POOR) QUALITY

The concept of *cost of quality* dates back to the early 1950s. It was introduced in Juran's *Quality Control Handbook* to show cost as a function of quality, expressed as conformance percentage. More detail about the material in this section can be found in Jack Campanella, editor, *Principles of Quality Costs,* 3rd Edition. Costs associated with quality are categorized into four different groupings:

- *Prevention.* The costs of all activities specifically designed to prevent poor quality in products or services.

- *Appraisal.* The costs associated with measuring, evaluating, or auditing products or services to assure conformance to quality standards and performance requirements.

- *Internal failure.* Costs resulting from products or services not conforming to requirements or customer/user needs. These occur prior to delivery or shipment of the product, or the furnishing of a service, to the customer.

- *External failure.* Costs resulting from products or services not conforming to requirements or customer/user needs. External failure costs occur after delivery or shipment of the product, and during or after the furnishing of a service, to the customer.

The first two categories are sometimes called the *cost of good quality,* and the last two are called the *cost of poor quality.* The sum of all of the categories is the *total quality costs.* It represents the difference between the actual cost of a product or service and what the reduced cost would be if there were no possibility of substandard service, failure of products, or defects in their manufacture.

While the premise of calculating costs of quality is straightforward, the execution of the calculations may not always be. Each identified quality problem carries with it a tangible recovery cost. But there are also intangible or "hidden" costs associated with the problems. They are often not as visible, either being buried in other accounting costs or not considered at all. These can often outweigh the visible costs. The commonly measured failure costs are merely the proverbial tip of the iceberg, with the bulk of failure costs below the surface. This analogy is shown in Figure 2.1.

Defects found by the customer are the most expensive of all. If the manufacturer or service provider had caught the defect, a less costly condition would result. If the manufacturing or service organization had been geared toward defect prevention and continuous quality improvement, defects and their resulting costs would have been minimized, the most desirable state. Historically, prevention and appraisal costs had been viewed as rising asymptotically as defect-free levels were achieved, leading to an optimal quality level for minimizing total quality cost. More recent thought is that prevention and appraisal costs (particularly prevention) increase as quality improves, but the increase is not asymptotic. Thus, the total quality

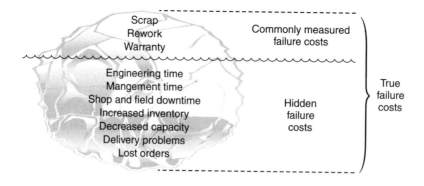

Figure 2.1 Hidden costs of quality and the multiplier effect.

Reproduced from Jack Campanella, editor, *Principles of Quality Costs,* 3rd Edition (Milwaukee: ASQ Quality Press, 1999): 7.

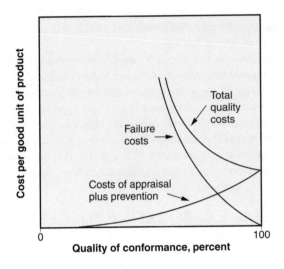

Figure 2.2 New model of optimum quality costs.
Reproduced from Jack Campanella, editor, *Principles of Quality Costs,* 3rd Edition (Milwaukee: ASQ Quality Press, 1999), 10.

cost is minimized when perfect quality is achieved, hence the drive for zero defects in both lean and Six Sigma. This is depicted in Figure 2.2.

The purpose of using quality costs is to facilitate quality improvement efforts that have a positive impact on the financial performance of the organization. Campanella suggests the following four-step strategy:

1. Take direct attack on failure costs in an attempt to drive them to zero

2. Invest in the "right" prevention activities to bring about improvement

3. Reduce appraisal costs according to results achieved

4. Continuously evaluate and redirect prevention efforts to gain further improvement

This strategy is based on three premises:

- For each failure there is at least one root cause

- Causes are preventable

- Prevention is always the cheapest option

These steps and approaches are completely compatible with and supportive of lean and Six Sigma philosophies.

In general, improvement can be made and translated into dollars by addressing failure costs first, as these are the most costly to the business as a whole. As quality improves, there can be an associated decrease in appraisal costs accompanied by a slight increase in prevention costs to sustain the improvements. There are many subcategories identified for each of the major cost-of-quality categories. You will find a listing of some of these at the end of the book in Appendix A. They should stimulate thinking about the cost linkages associated with Six Sigma and lean projects.

SOME EXAMPLES OF SUCCESSFUL IMPROVEMENT INITIATIVES

There are many examples of successful lean and Six Sigma projects. Here are just a few from a Fortune 500 company engaged in Lean Six Sigma deployment:

- Work was done on a specific defect on a manufactured product. The nonconformance level for this defect was reduced by 82 percent, the waste by 63 percent, and the downtime by 12 percent. This translated into a total savings of $112,000.

- Work was done to optimize the supply chain for a given product. The inventory cost was reduced by 34 percent, the labor costs by 38 percent, and the logistics (transportation) costs by $90,000, for a total savings of $347,000.

- A project examined travel and entertainment costs, looking for root causes of large expenses and appropriate solutions. Policy changes were made concerning the class of air travel permitted. Advanced booking was made mandatory, as well as requirements to take the low-fare providers. While these may seem obvious, such policies had not been in place. Savings were estimated at $2,400,000 per year.

Let's take a look at a hypothetical example to see how to estimate the value of an improvement project.*

---

* The hypothetical example was developed by James R. Cook of the Eastman Kodak Company.

Here's the current situation before the improvement project. The organization has inventory with a net book value of $10,000,000. It is housed in ten buildings that are 10,000 square feet each. The value of the inventory is equally distributed between buildings. Each building has five employees who each earn $4000 per month (burdened rate). The cost of maintenance and air conditioning is $1000 per month per building. The depreciation charge is $2000 per month (the company owns the buildings). The stated reason for the inventory level is that "we need a 10 percent safety stock since we really don't know what our customers want." It takes three days to pick, package, and ship the product. Stock replenishment is based on what is sold. Gross margin is 30 percent, SG&A is 15 percent, and, for the purposes of this example, the tax rate is zero percent.

The improvement process was extremely successful. By developing successful marketing plans and selling aging inventory that would have been written off, inventory was lowered by $1,500,000. Getting a better handle on customer wants eliminated the need for safety stock; the optimal inventory level is now considered to be $9,000,000. The inventory reduction has allowed the remaining inventory to be consolidated into nine buildings. The order fulfillment process has been streamlined and improved so that it can now be done in two days. It is projected that the organization's expenses will be under budget by $20,000 per year for the next two years.

Let's look at the value of the improvements in qualitative terms—that is, which financial area the improvements affect—and then assign dollar values to those improvements.

- Selling off inventory—this is accretive to the balance sheet, increases net income, and increases cash.

- Closing one warehouse building (people and air conditioning savings)—increases net income and increases cash.

- Maintaining optimal inventory level—lowers cash and dilutes the balance sheet.

- Eliminating the need for safety stock (thus making the optimal inventory level lower)—makes balance sheet more liquid as there is a smaller cash outlay to maintain the lower optimal level.

Some of the changes have no *direct* financial impact:

- Closing the warehouse (depreciation)—depreciation continues because the building is still an asset on the balance sheet (this item would be different if the company were to sell the building).

- Improvement of order fulfillment time—there is no change in head count and no increase in sales. There could be an argument that you would get one additional day of sales and cash at the end of the year. There is another argument that this will increase customer satisfaction; this has financial impact if intangibles are factored in with some model.

- Underrunning the budget—this could earn a pat on the back, but is not counted as hard dollar savings.

Now let's take a look at how we assign dollar values to these from a P&L, balance sheet, and cash flow perspective. The P&L components are shown in the Figure 2.3.

The top sheet shows the effect of the sale of inventory. If we sold $1,500,000 of book value, with a 30 percent gross margin, the revenues from

Details of P&L Calculation

Sale of Excess/Aging Inventory

P&L	
Revenue	$ 2,142,857
COGS	$ 1,500,000
Gross margin	$ 642,857
SG&A	$ 321,429
EFO	$ 321,428

Building Consolidation

P&L	
Revenue	$ —
COGS	$ —
Gross margin	$ —
SG&A	$ (252,000)
EFO	$ 252,000

Consolidated

P&L	
Revenue	$ 2,142,857
COGS	$ 1,500,000
Gross margin	$ 642,857
SG&A	$ 69,429
EFO	$ 573,428

Figure 2.3   The P&L statement for the improvements.

the sale are $2,142,857, giving a gross margin of $624,857 (that is, 70 percent of $2,142,857 is $1,500,000). The SG&A associated with that revenue is $321,429 (15 percent of the revenue) resulting in increased earnings of $321,428. The middle sheet shows the effect of consolidating the inventory into nine buildings. We no longer need to staff or air condition one building, so we save the salaries of $4,000 per month × five employees × 12 months, or $240,000, along with the air conditioning savings of $1,000 per month × 12 months, or $12,000. The total savings resulting from the consolidation is $252,000 for the year. Adjusting to an optimal inventory level has no effect on the P&L statement. The consolidated effects on the P&L statement are shown in the bottom sheet of the figure. The total hard dollar savings from sale of inventory and building consolidation is $573,428.

The balance sheet components are shown in Figure 2.4. We will assume a starting cash level of $1,000,000 (the figure is somewhat irrelevant since we will be looking at deltas). The top sheet shows the effect of the sale of inventory. Revenues were obtained in the form of cash, so $2,142,857 of cash

Details of Balance Sheet Calculation

Sale of Excess/Aging Inventory

Balance Sheet	YE 2004	YE 2005
Assets	Pre-Sale	Post-Sale
Cash	$ 1,000,000	$ 2,821,428
Inventory	$ 10,000,000	$ 8,500,000
Net current assets	$ 11,000,000	$ 11,321,428

Maintaining Optimal Inventory Level

Balance Sheet	YE 2004	YE 2005
Assets	Pre-Purchase	Post-Sale
Cash	$ 2,821,428	$ 2,321,428
Inventory	$ 8,500,000	$ 9,000,000
Net current assets	$ 11,321,428	$ 11,321,428

Consolidated

Balance Sheet	YE 2004	YE 2005
Assets	Start	Finish
Cash	$ 1,000,000	$ 2,321,428
Inventory	$ 10,000,000	$ 9,000,000
Net current assets	$ 11,000,000	$ 11,321,428

Figure 2.4 The balance sheet for the improvements.

came in, associated with an SG&A expense of $321,429 (cash going out). So the net cash in is $1,821,428. Selling the inventory reduced the inventory level from $10,000,000 to $8,500,000, or a decrease of $1,500,000. So the net positive effect from sale of inventory is $321,428.

Net cash earned – Value of inventory sold = Net positive effect
$1,821,428 – $1,500,000 = $321,428

At this point, the building consolidation has no impact on cash or inventory since it resulted in an empty, unsold building. Adjusting to optimal inventory will necessitate an increase in the inventory level from the current $8,500,000 to $9,000,000. The cost to produce the additional inventory reduces cash by $500,000. So the cash and inventory lines change, but the net current assets do not, as reflected in the middle sheet. The bottom sheet shows the consolidated effects, resulting in a soft dollar "savings" of $321,428.

The last category to consider is cash. This is already shown on the balance sheet. We saw a $1,821,428 increase in cash resulting from the sale of inventory and a $500,000 decrease in cash to adjust the inventory to its optimum level. So the net effect on cash was a $1,321,428 increase.

SOME GUIDELINES ON VALUING PROJECTS

Hopefully, the principles of converting improvements from process measures to financial measures seem relatively straightforward. The trick, of course, comes in the actual implementation. There are several lessons to be learned from companies who have been doing this for a while.

Decide on the Basis for Calculation. Project values can be expressed in terms of first-year savings, actual savings to date, or net present value (based on five years), just to name a few. First-year savings is likely the most common, with net present value being next. Choose one basis, and use that for all projects.

If You Don't Eliminate the Cost, Nothing Is Saved. This boils down to the difference between actual savings and paper savings, best explained with an example. Let's say an improvement project has been completed, the work flow has been improved, variation has been decreased, and the work that was done in eight hours can now be done in six hours. If everyone is kept on the payroll and there is no additional revenue-generating work that is done, the savings are theoretical and not real. In a growth business that is capacity-constrained, additional product can be manufactured and sold, so the dollars are there. The acid test is to establish a policy that the amount of expense savings claimed as a result of improvement projects will be deducted from the department's budget for the following year.

Solicit Finance Involvement. Best practices from companies implementing lean and Six Sigma initiatives show that people from the organization's finance department are involved in the valuation of improvement efforts. There are many reasons for doing this. One is that there will be greater consistency in the valuation across all departments since the finance people have the most knowledgeable background for the translation. Another is that finance people have the most direct access to systems that might have necessary information for performing the calculations such as labor rates, revenues, and so on). A third reason is the credibility lent to the process. There will always be people who will question and challenge the validity of the savings claimed. A formal sign-off by the department's finance person gives additional credibility to the stated amount.

Make a Decision About Soft, Intangible Improvements. Companies differ in their opinion and practice as to whether these improvements should be included in dollar amounts associated with lean and Six Sigma efforts. And there is no right answer. There have been many studies performed to validate the relationship between employee satisfaction and company success. Similarly, there have been many studies linking improved customer satisfaction to increased market share and revenue. So projects that result in improved employee satisfaction and customer satisfaction can be translated into dollars, making some assumptions. The decision needs to be made whether these should be included, and if so, what the rules of the road are for making the dollar conversion.

Be Consistent. This is probably the best advice of all. There can always be discussion about how to quantify improvement efforts. Which elements of cost of quality should be included? Do we include both hard and soft savings? What is the basis for reporting—first-year savings or net present value? What is important is having this discussion and coming up with an answer. The selected answer is less important than making the decision. And once the decision is made, it should be broadly communicated, understood, and adhered to.

3

Implementing Lean
Six Sigma

A journey of a thousand miles begins with a single step.

Confucius

I'M INTERESTED . . . NOW WHAT?

You've probably read this far because you suspect that your organization might gain a lot of value from lean and Six Sigma. Maybe it's time for a 'reality check.'

In fact, the journey toward a "Lean Six Sigma enterprise" is not one to undertake casually. Many resources are available to help you, however, and though the necessary commitment may be large it is still within reach for nearly any company.

What Help Is Available?

Starting with The American Society for Quality (ASQ), significant help is available, from publications through training and certification. Experienced and effective consultants have 'been there' and are available to help you get started as painlessly and cost-effectively as possible. Finally, professional groups and the Internet are making networking easy and valuable.

Let's explore these resources one at a time. Each of them may provide unique support to extend the reach of your commitment, perhaps beyond your expectations.

American Society for Quality

ASQ publishes numerous books and other publications on Six Sigma, and its lean collection is growing. These items are available at conferences or from the Society's Web site: www.asq.org. The Society also provides flexible training options in Six Sigma and lean enterprise. Typically, these courses are offered in larger cities, at conferences, or on-site if your facility has enough trainees. Six Sigma Green Belt and Black Belt training and certification are available, and the ASQ certifications for both are widely recognized.

Colleges and Universities

From community colleges, through university engineering and management programs, you may find local and affordable assistance for training. Online universities are providing lean and Six Sigma training as well. An Internet search should uncover schools that offer these courses in your geographic area.

Networks and Forums

Nothing beats the Internet when it comes to sharing experiences with your peers. What has worked for them? What advice would your peers offer you, and do you have anything valuable you would like to share? Public forums often contain featured articles as well as a message board.

One of the best and largest Six Sigma forums is a virtual community within ASQ, available for a nominal addition to your dues. ASQ also hosts a Lean Enterprise Forum.

Consultants

Consultants offer the skills, experience, and perspective needed to 'see around the corners' and assure that your implementation has the highest payback possible. Consultants are available to assist you in developing a strategy that will work. They can provide training, lead key projects as needed, and mentor your organization to achieve its goals.

Remember, a good consultant has been there. Lean and Six Sigma don't have to be difficult and complex but should be made to fit your organization's needs. While an off-the-shelf solution might work for you, a consultant could provide the perspective necessary for success.

How Large a Commitment Am I Making?

Lean Six Sigma is not just a set of quality and productivity improvement tools. More significantly, it requires a major cultural shift for most organizations. At the beginning of your implementation, the cost of human capital (resources) may be large. Nearly everyone in an organization will require some degree of training, whether just an introduction for employees not directly and immediately involved in initial projects or up to a month of classroom training for Black Belts/lean experts. Added up, there is no doubt the competition for human resources will be large, and your top management team must be trained first to assure that they will be able to support allocating the appropriate resources.

While it may be tempting to circumvent the up-front investment in training, this is highly discouraged. For an adequate cultural shift to take place, one that will provide and sustain the main benefits of your Lean Six Sigma program, everyone must understand and support the initiative. To be most valuable, Lean Six Sigma needs to be the way everyone works—from thinking to making decisions and then acting on them.

For larger companies especially, such as those where lean and Six Sigma won their first major successes, there was no other way to create the large-scale cultural understanding and shift other than to complete big investments in training up-front, across the board. However, mid- and small-sized companies are increasingly finding that they have other options. The right consultant can lead projects and get immediate financial payback while training by example and then following up with the full suite of tools. Small- and mid-sized companies can also take advantage of the many tools available from ASQ, forums, and the other sources already noted.

So most of the initial financial commitment will be in the form of training. Considering that the cost of training a Six Sigma Black Belt can be more than $10,000 plus travel expenses, the project plan must fully account for these costs. Additional financial commitments can include application software needed to run the necessary statistical calculations, such as MINITAB, Statsoft, or JMP, to name a few. And for start-up budgeting, don't forget the costs of regularly scheduled team meetings and reviews if your accounting system tracks these costs. Eventually, the ongoing costs of maintaining a Lean Six Sigma culture will shrink, with the benefits far exceeding the cost.

ISO 9000 and Other Quality System Investments

ISO 9000 and other standards define what a business must do to establish and control its processes. Lean Six Sigma methodology adds the all-important "how to" recipe for making performance breakthroughs.

ISO 9000, lean, and Six Sigma are much stronger together than any one of them alone. You will be able to use your quality management system to define, measure, and enforce (control) the improvements you will make through your projects.

However, you might find that your leadership group needs specific training regarding these synergies. They might feel that the company has already made enough investment in quality. In your leadership training, you will need to make sure everyone understands that Lean Six Sigma is to be the operating philosophy and culture of your company, and as such, the investments already made in ISO 9000 will be used to their full benefit rather than abandoned.

You Don't "Do" Manufacturing? Not a Problem

The roots of lean and Six Sigma are in manufacturing, but today any organization that can define its work in terms of customer needs, process steps, inputs, outputs, and measurements will benefit.

For inspiration, look to the city of Fort Wayne, Indiana, which deployed Six Sigma in all departments from public safety to utilities and the City Council. (See Appendix B.) Lean Six Sigma is not just about reducing cost. Happier customers will provide rewards in the form of more sales, often directly linked to real improvements realized through lean and Six Sigma projects. Improvement projects can result in better-defined customer demographics as well as more highly valued products and services, no matter the industry.

If you can define a work process using flowcharts—and you can!— lean and Six Sigma are almost certain to help you, manufacturing or not. Even if you don't use flowcharts now, keep in mind the philosophy that all work is a process. And we can all improve our processes.

The Implications for Your Organization's Culture

Your organization's culture will have an impact on Lean Six Sigma implementation that can't be overemphasized. You will need to be armed and ready to persuade the hardened critics that you aren't undertaking just another fad.

In fact, without the process focus lean and Six Sigma will bring, your organization may be used to succeeding through the efforts of a few stand-out 'heroes.' The heroes know the ropes and are able to rally others to getting the job done, sometimes at the expense of valuable process discipline. But implementing Lean Six Sigma will reward those people who are able to measure and analyze processes and to make those processes highly reliable and efficient. The role of the hero will be replaced with a new reality of shared processes. Recognize that some of the organization's leaders will become early adopters and will be eager to help Lean Six Sigma succeed, while others will not make the transition to share in the power of process improvement. Other leaders more aligned with your new culture will emerge in your new environment.

Because of these dynamics, it is important to build reward systems for leaders and teams that are directly aligned with both top business goals and completion of meaningful process improvement projects. Employees need to see in a tangible way that lean and Six Sigma are not fads for your organization but rather your core strategy for breakthrough improvements.

When Should You Expect to Realize the Benefits?

Very early in your implementation, probably just after your first introductory training, getting everybody thinking about process improvement at the same time will cause an avalanche of easy ideas. This 'ground fruit' is easy to pick up and benefit from.

Yes, your organization will be trained in rigorous methodologies, project teams will be assembled, meetings and reviews will follow, and so on. All of this structure is important to get to the 'higher fruit' up the tree of success. However, it is very important to get the easy improvements right away. If the improvement makes immediate sense, go ahead and just do it! Nothing could be a surer death knell than your organization perceiving lean and Six Sigma to be bureaucratic exercises of going through motions before any real understanding and experience is obtained.

Make sure you go for the quick wins to demonstrate the success that can be gained through lean and Six Sigma. The scope and scale of your initial projects need to be carefully defined to be both significant and doable in a relatively short time. Then make sure you widely celebrate and communicate the results and rewards as a model for more good things to come.

If your organization is typical, you'll see some immediate improvements. More substantial improvements will probably require the first wave of new projects to be completed in two to four months, followed by additional projects.

GETTING STARTED

Lean, Six Sigma, or Both?

The question of where to start is not as baffling as it might seem. The answer lies in the types of projects your company will find most immediately beneficial, what you are trying to achieve with your suppliers and customers, and the readiness of your organization to act on these opportunities.

Which First? And Does it Matter?

Remember that the purpose of your first improvement projects is to create the conditions for cultural change as well as measurable and meaningful improvement to customer satisfaction, cost, speed, or other factors. Your choice of initial projects will determine which toolkit to use, though whichever you choose, it is important to just get started.

However, it is easiest to decide where to start if you remember that lean projects and Six Sigma projects can be used as complementary steps. For example, if the most immediate need is to improve the cycle time of an operation, error-proof certain steps, or better organize work flow, the natural place to start would be with a lean project. If the process is already organized and in control and now the customer is more interested in reducing the variation in on-time shipments or product defects, Six Sigma would make sense. After that, you might discover that a certain process step requires too much work-in-process inventory to maintain uptime: back to lean.

Consider a Wide Variety of Improvement Needs, Then Choose Carefully

Your improvement needs should be strongly tied to the business strategic plan and be measurable. A list of potential projects should be generated and considered by the management team. Some strategy is in order here. While it is tempting to undertake a wide variety of projects, some lean, some Six Sigma, some both, across departments, and so on, this is usually not the most effective first course.

Instead, select an area of business that has a few critical goals and measurements that can be improved by using a group of projects that will readily support each other and give a synergistic result. Now, do these projects look like lean, Six Sigma, or both?

Save the rest of that list of great project ideas for the next round. In the first round of projects it is most important to demonstrate some great successes and then grow your implementation into other areas.

Consider Your Customers and Suppliers

Are you on the same team with your customers and suppliers? If so, what would make your organization perform better within the entire supply chain? You will gain a lot of goodwill by asking your customers and even involving them directly in your projects. Likewise, by educating your suppliers through some initial projects, you have the opportunity to improve the supply chain coming into your company. In fact, getting both your suppliers and customers involved in your effort will be essential in completing your Lean Six Sigma enterprise.

However, do not fall into the trap of demanding more from your suppliers than your own organization is willing and able to do. Your suppliers will judge the seriousness of your intent by the actions of your company. Setting the example by the quality, pace, and results of your projects will create inspiration rather than resentment. Indeed, when both your company and your suppliers succeed together, the benefits will be greatest. After all, when looking for process improvements, the best ones may often be found in the organizational interfaces.

Consider the Organization's Readiness

Do you already have experience in your organization with some of the tools of either lean or Six Sigma? If so, you should take advantage of this in your first selection of projects and resources. Does your company already see the need for speed in the process flow? This can be a great launching point for lean. Or does your company have employees with technical skills in statistics and process control who can harness the power of Six Sigma statistics right away? This could get Six Sigma off to an impressive start.

Planning to Succeed

Successful Lean Six Sigma starts with a detailed but flexible and realistic plan. The need to gain early understanding and commitment is high, and projects must be followed through with discipline as there are many pitfalls. Ultimately, everyone needs to be fully committed to a complete and thorough game plan.

A typical Lean Six Sigma implementation may progress through six distinct phases:

1. *Vision and communication.* A clear and compelling vision must be identified, communicated, and accepted by stakeholders. What is the desired outcome for the projects, for the business, and for the customer? What financial benefits must be achieved to justify the commitment to Lean Six Sigma? What measurable benefits will customers see in cost, speed, and quality?

2. *Focus, structure, and education.* Since effective teamwork is essential for successful projects, training in roles and responsibilities is as important as technical skills development. Cohesive, cross-functional teams need to be nurtured. Supportive Champions are critical to this process and should be able to remove obstacles; teams must see their project as

a significant business priority. Black Belts and Green Belts, who may serve several teams, should receive training in project management and creating cultural change, as appropriate. All team members will need to dedicate time and effort to make their projects successful and will benefit from continuous reinforcement of their efforts and unique roles.

3. *Define key metrics.* A system of metrics, or key performance indicators, will show progress in fulfilling the vision of the implementation and achieving specific goals. This system should be established early in implementation since projects should be selected to improve these indicators collectively. Examples of key performance indicators are shown in Table 3.1.

4. *Basic Lean Six Sigma tool deployment.* Early projects may require only the essentials of lean and Six Sigma and provide the quick and tangible results that an organization needs to gain experience and build enthusiasm. Just-in-time using visual controls and standardized work is a good starting point. 5S (sort, set in order, shine, standardize, sustain) will get the ball rolling toward a highly productive work space. With Six Sigma, process mapping, classification of defects and causes, and basic hypothesis testing and data analysis may be all that are needed for initial projects.

5. *Advanced tool deployment.* As teams gain experience, more advanced methods such as cellular manufacturing, total productive maintenance, mistake-proofing, kanban, design of experiments, and advanced statistics may be appropriate. Black Belts, in particular, will need a practical and thorough understanding of process capability and optimization. The rewards for using the advanced tools may include exciting breakthroughs and discoveries that will energize the project teams further and identify new project ideas.

Table 3.1   Examples of key performance indicators.

Quality	Cost	Delivery	Safety
• Scrap • First-pass yield • DPMO/sigma level • Process capability	• Labor $/unit • Cost of poor quality • Inventory turns • WIP value	• OEE (overall equipment effectiveness) • On time delivery • MTBF (mean time between failures) • MTTR (mean time to repair)	• OSHA RIR (reportable incident rate) • Near misses • 5S compliance • Employee training compliance

6. *Transfer to entire value stream.* After success is achieved in a business unit or department with the basic tools of Lean Six Sigma, the implementation process will need to be transferred to other areas. Advanced tools may also be employed at this point where initial projects require them. Best practices and methodologies should be documented and communicated to make the implementation as customized and relevant as possible.

Great Project Management Is a Must!

The need for successful implementation cannot be overemphasized. If the leaders of your initiative need project management training, you need to recognize this as a critical set of skills and build this aspect of training into the plan.

Initially, you will probably have an enthusiastic crowd to work with. However, as projects unfold there will be an increasing number of commitments to make. Certain individuals may tire of the rigor required or the perceived conflict with day-to-day work.

For many companies, the best way to counteract these problems is to use formal project planning methods, including PERT and Gantt charts. If you use these tools with discipline, the ongoing accountability and commitment you need will be managed accurately, properly, and well.

Still, when the implementation schedule starts to slip, as inevitably it will, you are going to have to use the 'people' side of your project management skills. The critical skills will shift from an emphasis on technical expertise, and success will depend heavily on the sincerity and depth of top management's commitment. Nurture this commitment thoroughly and continuously.

Getting Management Commitment

Sooner or later in your implementation, the level of management commitment you achieve will profoundly affect the outcome. Be aware of the possibility that some cautious or skeptical leaders who at first do not appear to support your efforts may later turn out to be your biggest allies once they see tangible results, while others who feign support in the beginning might end up sabotaging the effort later when they realize the level of commitment required.

Three of the best ways to assure management support are to:

- Provide early training focused on setting up expectations for clear business results and measurements

- Align projects to support the needs of each key manager's department, for example, provide a personal interest

- Insist on frank and open discussion about the progress of implementation

When it's time to celebrate success, make sure that both the leaders who provide the resources and the members of the Lean Six Sigma project teams are all recognized and rewarded.

Leveraging "The Language of Business"

Make sure that your plan is couched in the language of business—dollars and cents, cycle times, inventory turns, return on investment, and so on. Even customer satisfaction can be translated into these terms. When a Lean Six Sigma project is consuming resources that can be measured in these terms, it is vital to show the potential or actual benefits the same way.

Think Big

Make sure that the organization establishes challenging or 'breakthrough' goals. The means of reaching those goals will depend on solutions that won't be obvious at first or you would have instituted them already. For example, a goal to "reduce inventory from $2.0 million to $1.9 million" will not get as much support as "reduce inventory by 50 percent" or even 90 percent. This is where the value of Lean Six Sigma comes in, and obviously it's going to take some new thinking!

Avoid any projects that do not directly impact a top-level business goal. At the same time, you have to keep in mind that in order to make noticeable progress on a top-level goal, more than one or two projects may be required. Your best guide is to make each project small enough to be achievable in a reasonable time with budgeted resources while synergizing with like projects to make a measurable impact on those top goals.

Use Metrics and Dashboards

Metrics, dashboards, and so on—what's the fuss all about? You want to create a culture where every person in the organization has a clear line of sight, through metrics they directly influence, to the top business goals. The top goals for an area in your business may be summarized in a dashboard and made highly visible to everyone—customers and suppliers included! A sample dashboard is shown in Figure 3.1.

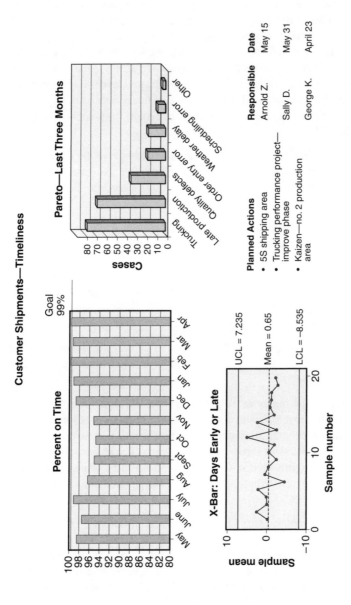

Figure 3.1 Dashboard example for a shipping function.

Metrics are actually the lifeblood of your improvement program. Spend time carefully defining them within your project teams. Eventually the metrics themselves will become part of the language of your business, and people at all levels will strive to improve them continually. Remember, metrics are ultimately just indicators; it is impossible for any one metric to tell the whole truth. When a metric has outlived its usefulness, go ahead and get rid of it! As your organization completes projects and learns more and more of the truth, this kind of flexibility will be absolutely necessary.

Effective metrics have several characteristics, summarized by the acronym SMART:

Simple. Will most employees be able to quickly grasp the meaning of the metric without lots of theoretical explanation? You could measure fuel efficiency in terms of 'pounds of gasoline per horsepower per hour,' but 'miles per gallon' just makes sense.

Measurable. Do you have a clear and reliable way to determine the parameter you are considering? For instance, "customer loyalty" can be difficult to assess over typical measuring periods of a few weeks or months. Specific elements of customer satisfaction, however, are measurable with well-constructed surveys. You may prefer to measure satisfaction even though it does not always guarantee loyalty.

Achievable. The goal must be challenging but not be so high that it is unrealistic. A company that has maintained 22 percent market penetration for many years may be able to excite employees to beat 30 percent, but 60 percent could be folly.

Realistic. Is the outcome truly within the control of the employees who will be using the metric and does it make sense to them? Overall customer satisfaction with your product may not be a realistic measure or improvement area for the sales force—there are many factors outside of their control influencing this metric. On the other hand, time to close or process a sale, which may contribute to overall customer satisfaction, may be very appropriate.

Timely. The metric must be produced and distributed frequently to be useful. Consider that if you are trying to achieve a quarterly goal, the metric should be produced at least monthly. If a monthly goal, consider weekly metrics, and so on. This strategy will prevent surprises and allow midcourse correction so that teams get in the habit of meeting goals—one of the tangible cultural changes you probably want to achieve.

How Many Sigmas Make Sense?

One objection you are likely to encounter is that "we don't make a million of anything," and you'll have to be armed with an answer. Six sigma, the theoretical attainment of near perfection (3.4 defects per million), isn't the literal goal but rather a concept for excellence.

Your company may be used to measuring things in percentages, for instance. If the yield is 98.5 percent, then you have 1.5 percent defects, or 15,000 defects per million. This is equivalent to 3.7 sigma. If, after consulting with your customers, your company sets a goal of 0.5 percent defects this year, your target is 5000 defects per million, or 4.1 sigma.

Whether you measure this change in sigma or percentages, you are striving for a threefold reduction. But in the language of Six Sigma, moving from one sigma level to another demands substantial change. Remember, you are striving for breakthroughs. No matter what process you are optimizing, the quality level can be expressed consistently and compared directly to other processes as long as all of them are expressed as a sigma level.

Lean Concepts

Lean uses yet another set of terms and concepts. Some of the key ones, such as value stream, waste, and cycle time, are discussed in the previous chapters.

From an implementation viewpoint, the main concern is that these terms should be clearly understood and used the same way by everyone in the organization. Your training plan and communications scheme should be designed to establish this common understanding, lest anyone feel left behind by the 'mumbo jumbo' of it.

Defining Projects of Significant Value

Selection of the best initial improvement projects will create increasing interest in Lean Six Sigma, provide substantial and visible results, and set the stage for the next round of projects. Initial projects, therefore, need to be "quick hits" whenever possible and need to involve all of the key areas of the organization.

As stated earlier, projects are usually determined by the leadership of the organization and should be designed to accomplish the strategic goals of the company. The leadership team should include the lean or Six Sigma expert or a Master Black Belt and will need to start by defining a process for project selection. This is called a *project funnel* and may be refined over time, but it is important to establish a process that will assure a uniform evaluation against selection criteria. Developing and using a project funnel will prevent inappropriate projects from being selected on the basis of old paradigms, current hierarchies, and so on.

Project charters are frequently used as a way of providing both input and output to the project selection process. In a charter, a proposed project must be defined and submitted to the leadership team or the project selection team. The charter should include:

- A title for the project

- The business organization or areas and strategic goals that the project will impact

- A summary description of the current state and future state of the process

- The business impact of the project

- A proposed project team and timeline

The current state should include the key metric to be improved and its current value. In order to be meaningful, initial projects should stretch for a dramatic improvement. Later, as opportunities diminish in a business area, a smaller reduction would be appropriate. Of course, the means of achieving the reduction are not yet known or presented in the charter, but it is important to establish goals for the future state nonetheless. The charter is submitted to the leadership team for formal approval. Any proposed charters that are not chosen as first projects will form a library for future ideas.

Project leaders should possess excellent communication and leadership skills. It is not necessary that the leader be the ultimate "expert" in the area to be improved. In fact, projects need to be approached with an open mind. Effective project teams will typically contain five to eight members. The team members should represent the suppliers, users, and customers of the process to be improved, and the team as a whole should contain an all-around knowledge of the important technical or operational factors in the project. Finally, the project team needs to have adequate credibility and authority.

Providing resources to project teams is not a matter to be taken lightly. In nearly every organization there will be contention for these same resources, and day-to-day work must still be accomplished even as the project gets under way. Therefore, the time requirements for each member must be estimated in advance according to the project schedule, and commitment for this time must be obtained both from each employee and his or her manager.

Communications

Communications will need to occur frequently and consistently at several levels of detail: top-level program status, leadership review, and the status of individual team projects. An effective Lean Six Sigma implementation should have a plan indicating what types of communications are to occur (meetings, video, and so on), who the audiences will be, who has the responsibility for the communication, and due dates. A simple matrix will suffice, identifying the types of planned communications in a left-hand column, followed by the elements of each in rows. No matter how the plan is laid out, the important point will be to implement it consistently.

Top-level program communications can take various forms: employee meetings, company newsletters, company events to celebrate success, and even parts of the training program such as all-employee training on the basics of Lean Six Sigma.

Leadership review of all projects should occur at least monthly, while review of the status of the overall program should happen at least quarterly. Of course, these time frames are guidelines and should be adjusted as needed. The point is that these reviews will assure that the program stays on track and responds to changes in business strategy that may occur from time to time, and that project teams continue to be held accountable.

Shortly after their introduction to Lean Six Sigma, most employees will be wondering how projects are proceeding. The key information to be communicated includes all of the information in the project charters plus frequent updates for each project on the improvement to date, the current phase of the project, the estimated completion date, and anything else of general interest. Remember that employees outside of the defined team may provide additional valuable input and, even if that doesn't happen, they need frequent and specific communication to help them buy into Lean Six Sigma.

Training

The training program will need to include all employees, from top management through the Belts and experts (however you define their title), improvement team members, the organization at large, and suppliers and customers. Where training systems already exist, such as a training organization or just a training database, Lean Six Sigma training should be integrated into those same systems. Your company will also need to decide whether to certify its Belts and experts formally, and if so, how to do this.

Management training will need to provide leaders and managers an insightful and condensed introduction to Lean Six Sigma principles, the benefits and costs the organization anticipates, and a road map for full implementation. For top managers, this training can be accomplished in as little as a half day, but it will need to be done before all other training. For those leaders who will be directly involved in the implementation or project reviews (sometimes called Champions), two days of training is generally appropriate. The additional training time will allow these leaders to fully engage in the strategic aspects of Lean Six Sigma and help bring about the desired cultural changes through demonstrating Lean Six Sigma support in everyday decision making.

Training for the Lean Six Sigma Belts, or "experts" if this title is preferred, requires the most significant investment. For a typical Black Belt, 20 days of classroom training is typically conducted in segments over a four-month period. In addition, the Black Belt trainees are often expected to lead and complete a demonstration project. Green Belts can be trained with much less classroom training but might still be required to complete a demonstration project. Candidates for Green Belt training must have credibility within the organization as change leaders, excellent communication skills, and an intellectual capacity for the rigors of the methodologies, especially as they relate to statistics. Your company might want to include college-level math as a prerequisite for these trainees. Team members will need an introduction to the tools of Lean Six Sigma but without the advanced methods. This training may vary in length according to your organization's needs and the existing skills of the team members, from one-half day to a full week.

Finally, the organization at large will require an introduction to Lean Six Sigma. You should expect to spend approximately two hours describing the expectations for implementation and the roles each employee may have in it. While this might sound like a lot of time spent for the entire organization, it gives you the opportunity to plant the seeds for the cultural transformation that truly will involve everyone.

Your organization might want to include formal certification as part of its training program. ASQ offers certifications for Six Sigma Black Belt (CSSBB) and Six Sigma Green Belt (CSSGB). The ASQ certifications are widely recognized. If you use a consulting company for your training, that company might offer its own certification that indicates training has been completed and possibly that a project has been completed. These types of certification programs vary in their content as there are currently no established standards on this type of training/certification. Despite this, however, most certification programs are similar in key aspects such as the areas of knowledge and proficiency that must be demonstrated. Perhaps even more importantly, these types of certification provide an additional and important recognition that serves to motivate employees to succeed.

Project Implementation

Okay, you've got an improvement project to lead. Let's get started. It's time to bring out the best project management skills you have, because you are going to need them! Besides being a taskmaster to drive the specific parts of the schedule, you will need to ensure accountability and rewards for your team. You also need to get your project through the reviews or 'gates' that will keep it on track and ultimately successful. Finally, you'll need to leave controls in place to assure that your improvements continue after the project is done.

Guidelines for a Lean Six Sigma Project

When considering a Lean Six Sigma project, keep in mind that tools from both the lean and the Six Sigma domains can be used. Both lean and Six Sigma borrow a lot from total quality management (process mapping, Pareto charts, fishbone charts or Ishikawa diagrams, and much more). Lean is rich in tools such as value stream mapping, 5S, and all the others previously described, and often uses kaizen as the way to get a team together to accomplish improvements in less than a week. Six Sigma adds statistical tools and a powerful overarching methodology: define–measure–analyze–improve–control (DMAIC), and this approach can require three to six months of teamwork to institute some of the more profound process changes needed.

We'll illustrate this point with a typical project that uses lean and Six Sigma in effective combination. Let's say our fictional company, Acme, provides mortgages to consumers. It provides both products and services, since it assists customers through the mortgage application process and also produces the actual mortgage through its internal production operations.

Where should we start? Which tools would Acme use?

Acme started by listening to its customers, both lending banks and individual consumers, and examined their input in relation to its own strategic goals. Acme noticed several different kinds of problems:

1. The cycle time of a mortgage approval was two days longer than what their customers said they really wanted.

2. Lots of paperwork was being lost in Acme's underwriting step.

3. Bank customers were complaining that there was too much variation in the default rate of loans three years after closing.

4. Acme recognized there were too many errors in the mortgage paperwork, the company's physical product.

Acme realized there was no single solution to this wide variety of problems and set up four teams to recommend how to proceed. After reviewing their teams' project charters, Acme management approved the four projects, provided training, and set up a series of project reviews.

The first team worked on Acme's cycle time problem—two days longer than customers wanted. When the team starting mapping out the basic mortgage application, approval, and production processes, it realized that at many places in the process the paperwork was sitting in queue for the next operation. The team produced a value stream map and identified all the points of paperwork inventory at each step. As you will recall, one of the key features in a value stream map is to identify value-added and non-value-added (NVA) steps. The team wanted to eliminate NVA from the value stream: that is, any tasks that the customer is not willing to pay for, do not add features, or do not make Acme more competitive. The team determined that only two percent of the process cycle consisted of value-added activities used in processing the mortgage. So, from the customer's viewpoint, fully 98 percent of Acme's cycle time was wasted! The team held a one-week kaizen event in which they completely removed steps from day-to-day jobs and eliminated several of the queues by letting downstream operations schedule the steps supplying them. This team successfully eliminated three days of cycle time—50 percent better than the two-day reduction customers said they wanted—and identified several additional projects for the future. Some of these projects were destined to use lean tools, others Six Sigma, and still others both.

The second team worked on the problem of lost paperwork in the underwriting step. Here, lots of paperwork comes together from different parts of the application process as the underwriters attempt to make good decisions under difficult deadlines. Since underwriting is one of the last steps in the mortgage process, the underwriters felt like paperwork was being dropped on them from all directions. And to look at the actual desktops in the underwriting department you would conclude the same thing! The second team correctly realized that application of 5S would probably do a lot of good: sort, set in order, shine, standardize, sustain. The team started by *sorting* active mortgage loan applications from piles of unrelated paperwork, then disposed of unrelated paperwork and sent inactive files to archive. Next the team *set in order* by setting up "a place for everything and everything in its place," as the saying goes. The team cleaned up the work space to set a new standard and improve morale (*shine*). The team then went on to *standardize* the work flow, which included rearranging some of the desks in the underwriting department. Finally, procedures were put in place to *sustain* the improvement. The team accomplished this all within two weeks and there was never again a complaint about lost paperwork.

The third team had a very different kind of problem: banks were complaining that there was too much variation in the loan default rate. They didn't use those words, of course, but they said that if they knew with more certainty about the default risk (which is determined by Acme's underwriting department) for a given loan, they could apply a more appropriate interest rate for that loan. The team recognized that they were dealing with a variation problem, which is a statistics problem, and that Six Sigma might be the best way to accomplish improvement. This team went through the full DMAIC process of Six Sigma. One of the major findings was that the database of risk factors used to evaluate loan applicants needed a major upgrade. The team used design of experiments (DOE) and came up with a much better model of the risk profile for various types of mortgage applicants. This project took four months but it had a major business impact that was visible to everyone in Acme's organization and all of its customers.

The fourth team worked on the problem of too many errors in the mortgage paperwork. This paperwork, of course, is highly visible to customers. The team used Six Sigma DMAIC to map the process, to define specifically what is meant by "defects in the paperwork," and to get customer input on the metrics and goals that would demonstrate improvement. Using hypothesis testing, the team found that the second shift performed better than first shift, and then went on to discover and prove that this was due to a difference in training programs. Standard training was developed and delivered to all employees. The team also found a lot of problems that could be reduced or eliminated by error-proofing the forms and computer data inputs. And because the second team had fixed the problem of lost paperwork in the underwriting department through the use of 5S, errors were reduced even further.

At the completion of each project, Acme leadership made sure to reward the team members, communicate the successes far and wide, and use these success points as yet another opportunity to plant the seeds of cultural change the company was striving for.

How You Will Know Your Organization Is Finally a Lean Six Sigma Enterprise

Your organization may gradually extend Lean Six Sigma until it encompasses all business processes, not just operations. However, to truly be an enterprise, Lean Six Sigma must become ingrained in the way your organization actually works. Gradually the lines will blur between day-to-day work and improvement projects: improvement will become your organization's way of doing business. But beyond even these important cultural changes, you will know you have built a Lean Six Sigma enterprise when your suppliers and customers are also engaged in your success as your company's partners and mutual beneficiaries. In theory this is a journey that never ends but one that, in practice, many companies have already made.

Alternatives for Smaller Organizations

While it might seem that lean and Six Sigma are reserved for the province of large companies according to traditional ways of implementation, smaller companies are also doing well with them today. Indeed small companies even enjoy certain advantages. Smaller organizations need to follow the same flow of implementation as outlined above but they may have more acute human and financial capital constraints than large companies. When the typical employee wears many hats, it is unlikely a company can reserve very many (or any) positions for Lean Six Sigma experts.

What can be done to make implementation most practical and immediately beneficial? Smaller organizations have the edge of speed and agility over larger ones. In addition, lasting cultural change can be started with just a relatively few highly successful projects. In this scenario, experienced consultants who can assist with completion of real projects can be a great supplement to lean and Six Sigma training projects.

Customizing the project plan to fit a small organization's resources will go a long way to improve management and employee acceptance. Depending on the projects initially chosen, it might not be necessary to train teams to use all of the tools that could conceivably work for each step in the methodology. It might be better to train the team in basic tools and follow up with more advanced training as projects require.

Smaller organizations in particular don't often have the luxury of dedicated expert resources. Here the risk is especially great that management and employees will perceive Six Sigma as 'add-on work.' A smaller organization must be careful to not shortchange the importance of excellent metrics and reward systems, lest the critical momentum be overrun by firefighting activities.

If a smaller organization enters into Lean Six Sigma with these concerns in mind, identifies plans to addresses them, and follows through, its opportunities for success are bright.

Alternatives for Nonmanufacturing Organizations

Although lean and Six Sigma are often perceived as being designed for manufacturing, these tools and approaches have been used in nonmanufacturing environments such as service industries with great success. How have they done it?

Success in the service sector starts with the realization that a process is a process. Whether manufacturing a brake drum, engineering a new design, or even processing checks at a bank, all work flows can be envisioned as processes. All have suppliers, inputs, processes, outputs, and customers (the SIPOC model) that can be defined and measured. The first challenge in this environment will be to train people to see everything they do as a process to be continually improved, and to drive out blame and frustration. Lean and Six Sigma are perfect for that.

A lot of the literature and training materials are still written in the language of manufacturing and this could be a problem for some. The training materials must be in the language of the business you are working in, and all training examples must be relevant. Remember that you're asking people to grasp a lot of new concepts in their training and initial project; it's too much to expect trainees to translate this abstract knowledge into their own environment. Take the time necessary to get the training materials customized and right for your organization.

For nonmanufacturers, it is especially important to find good examples outside of their own organization and use them to illustrate success. Fortunately, there are more and more examples every day. You can find them in the ASQ forums and publications.

GROWING YOUR SUCCESS

Learning from Other Organizations

Forums and networking are a great way to accelerate your Lean Six Sigma initiative. If your facility is one of several in your company, you may also benefit richly by setting up and leveraging project successes from one part of your company to another.

Beyond your own company, find out which competitors and partners are the best in the world at the things you are trying to achieve. How does your company measure up to them from your customer's point of view? What makes your competitors and partners particularly successful? Wherever you can measure the gap by benchmarking in this way, you are bound to find even more solutions to adopt. You probably don't have enough time to reinvent everything, do you?

Although the specifics may vary depending on the project and your business goals, fundamentally you are likely to find many solutions just by looking around, sharing, and then applying the same principles of a successful project to your organization.

Highly successful implementations have a formal way of spreading knowledge of high-payback projects as far and wide as possible and then extending the solutions to similar situations. You will know your implementation is mature when your organization is able to do this.

SHARING YOUR SUCCESSES

One way to "spread your successes far and wide" is with the technology of project tracking software. Enterprisewide systems are now available. They provide access and visibility to complete project documentation, starting with the project charter through to the metrics devised to assure that the project improvements remain in place and continue to yield success. Project tracking software is continually changing and improving. However, the best of the programs can take all of the communication and project management aspects of lean and Six Sigma implementation and automate much of the more tedious work.

A FINAL WORD

You are about to undertake Lean Six Sigma and are anxious for your company to achieve great things. Congratulations! Remember that building a culture of fun and energy will be vital for going beyond your early successes and sustaining them. You have lots of resources to help you along your journey. We wish you an exciting one.

Appendix A
Cost of Quality Items

PREVENTION

- *Customer/user perception surveys.* Programs to determine customer expectations and needs

- *Contract/document review.* Review and evaluation of customer contracts affecting actual product or service requirements

- *Field trials.* Planned observations and evaluation of end-product performance in trial situations

- *Supplier reviews.* Surveys to review and evaluate individual suppliers' capabilities to meet quality requirements

- *Supplier quality planning.* Planning for the incoming and source inspections and tests necessary to determine acceptance of supplier products

- *Operations quality planning.* Development of necessary product or service inspection, test, and audit procedures, appraisal documentation system, and workmanship or appearance standards to assure continued achievement of acceptable quality results

- *Operator quality education.* Development and conduct of formal operator training programs for the express purpose of preventing errors

Extracted from Jack Campanella, editor, *Principles of Quality Costs,* 3rd Edition (Milwaukee: ASQ Quality Press, 1999): Appendix B.

- *Quality system audits.* Audits performed to observe and evaluate the overall effectiveness of the quality management system and procedures

APPRAISAL

- *Receiving or incoming inspections.* All normal or routine inspection and/or testing of purchased materials, products, and services

- *Setup inspections and tests.* All setup or first-piece inspections and tests used to ensure that each combination of machine and tool is properly adjusted to produce acceptable products before the start of each production lot

- *Measurement equipment.* Acquisition (depreciation or expense), calibration, and maintenance of measurement or process control equipment

- *Maintenance and calibration labor.* All inspections, calibration, maintenance, and control of appraisal equipment, instruments, and gages used for evaluation of processes, products, or services for conformance to requirements

- *Field performance evaluations.* All appraisal efforts (inspections, tests, audits, and appraisal support activities) planned and conducted at the site for installation and/or delivery of large, complex products or the conduct of merchandised services

INTERNAL FAILURE

- *Purchased material reject disposition costs.* Disposal or sorting of incoming inspection rejects, including reject documentation, review and evaluation, disposition orders, handling, and transportation

- *Supplier corrective action.* Company-sponsored failure analyses and investigations into the cause of supplier rejects to determine necessary corrective actions; includes cost of visits to supplier locations for this purpose and cost to provide necessary added inspection protection while the problem is being resolved

- *Disposition costs.* Review and disposition of nonconforming product or service

- *Troubleshooting or failure analysis costs.* Failure analysis (physical, chemical, and so forth) conducted by or obtained from outside laboratories in support of defect cause identification

- *Operations corrective action.* Corrective actions taken to remove or eliminate the root causes of nonconformances identified for correction; includes rewriting operator instructions, redevelopment of processes or procedures, redesign or modification of equipment or tooling, and development and implementation of specific training needs

- *Operations rework and repair costs.* Labor, material, and overhead associated with rework or repair of defective product or service discovered within the operations process

- *Rework.* Material, labor, and burden for all work done to bring nonconforming product or service up to an acceptable condition

- *Repair.* Material, labor, and burden for all work done to bring nonconforming product up to an acceptable or equivalent but still nonconforming condition

- *Reinspection/retest costs.* That portion of inspection, test, and audit labor that is incurred because of rejects; includes documentation of rejects, reinspection or test after rework/repair, and sorting of defective lots

- *Scrap costs.* Material, labor, and overhead for defective product or service that is wasted or disposed of because it can not be reworked to conform to requirements

- *Downgraded end product or service.* Price differential between normal selling price and reduced selling price due to nonconforming or off-grade end products or services because of quality reasons

EXTERNAL FAILURE

- *Complaint investigations/customer or user service.* Investigating, resolving, and responding to individual customer or user complaints or inquiries, including necessary field service

- *Returned goods.* Evaluating and repairing or replacing goods not meeting acceptance by the customer or user due to quality problems

- *Recall costs.* Recall activity due to quality problems

- *Warranty claims.* Claims paid to the customer or user, after acceptance, to cover expenses, including repair costs such as removing defective hardware from a system or cleaning costs due to a food or chemical service accident

- *Liability costs.* Liability claims, including the cost of product or service liability insurance

- *Customer/user goodwill.* Costs incurred, over and above normal selling costs, to customers or users who are not completely satisfied with the quality of a delivered product or service, such as costs incurred because customers' quality expectations are greater than what they received

- *Lost sales.* Value of contribution margin lost due to sales reduction because of quality problems

Appendix B

Case Study #1: Fort Wayne, Indiana— Applying Lean Six Sigma to City Government

BACKGROUND

In 2000, the city of Fort Wayne, Indiana, like many communities, was facing increasing costs, diminishing satisfaction with public services, and increasingly limited resources. In addition, the city was confronting the challenges of increasing population and land area, decreased revenue, increased demands for services, rising state and federal mandates, and the threats posed by tornadoes, floods, and terrorism. City officials found themselves fixing the same problems every year and quickly realized that these problems could not be fixed with outdated ideologies. In a move unprecedented for city government and through the leadership and vision of Mayor Graham Richard, Fort Wayne embarked on a Six Sigma initiative to "bring a high-powered private sector program to government, enhance services for Fort Wayne citizens, and create a culture of renewed enthusiasm among employees to do their jobs better."[1]

Mayor Richard's vision for building a high performance city included linking Six Sigma to the city's strategic focus to retain and create jobs and leverage talent, technology, training, and tools through imagination, investment, and innovation. To help deploy this strategy, the Northeast Indiana TQM Network was formed, an alliance comprising over 40 large and small manufacturing, service, and nonprofit organizations. Participating firms shared a common interest in cost-effective training, a strong desire to learn from the experience of others, and a willingness to share information and ideas. At the onset of Fort Wayne's Six Sigma initiative, a two-day executive leadership training event was conducted to emphasize collaborative learning, continuous quality improvement, and a shared vision for change. The training focused on key topics such as customer focus, service improvement and measurement, and data-based decision making. Resulting action plans included creating a quality leadership council, appointing a full-time quality manager, and hiring a retired Master Black Belt from GE to assist in project selection.

Initially, the city's decision-making processes were largely based on opinion, not data. Available data was impeded by "noise," rendering it less meaningful. Adopting the Six Sigma tools required expert opinions to be supported with data, allowed problems to be solved by root cause analysis, and separated meaningless noise from the actual signal contained in raw data. Utilizing statistical tools such as control charts enabled city employees to distinguish between common and assignable cause variation, saving significant time and expense.

By August 2004, Fort Wayne quality practitioners realized that the Six Sigma tools do not lend themselves to all situations, and concurrently initiated a lean approach. Each month, two to four kaizen events were performed to help bring about rapid change and reduce non-value-added activity by identifying and eliminating the seven forms of waste. Tools such as process and value stream mapping were used to examine the flow of materials, information, and the number of man-hours associated with completing various tasks.

SUCCESS STORIES

The City of Fort Wayne is using Lean Six Sigma to initiate improvements in a number of different departments including community development, water pollution control, human resources, and solid waste management among others.[2] Following are just a few examples of how Lean Six Sigma has resulted in reduced costs, increased profits, and improved customer service:

- Between 2003 and 2005, the value of street lighting inventory was reduced $400,000 by putting an inventory system in place, reducing overstock, and improving order accuracy.

- Driving accident rates with associated costs and lost days were reduced to industry-best standards at Fort Wayne's water pollution control and filtration plant.

- Wastewater treatment plant performance was improved, resulting in a reduction of 100 tons of pollutants draining into local rivers. An annual cost savings of $280,000 was realized, while a $1.7M expenditure was avoided.

- The average cycle time to repair potholes in city streets was reduced from 48 hours in 2000 to 2.5 hours in 2004. Subsequently, responses to pothole complaints were reduced from 21 to three hours on average.

- The site plan development process was simplified, from 31 steps and seven man-hours per routing to seven steps and 2.25 man-hours.

- From 1996 to 2006, Fort Wayne experienced increases in the miles of maintained streets, miles of water and sewer mains, utility accounts, and city population. All of this was achieved while public works staffing levels decreased eight percent.

- Public works property tax funds savings totaled $2.9M, while water filtration plant operational savings equaled $450,000.

- The disposition rate of robbery cases has increased by 48 percent.

- Missed trash pickups were reduced by 50 percent.

- The number of miles of road repaved annually has doubled.

- Waiting time for building permit applications has been reduced from 47 to 12 days.

- Fire code reinspections increased by 23 percent and the average number of days to receive a reinspection has been reduced from 51 to 34.

- Homes, schools, and businesses were wired via fiber optics to improve Internet literacy, enable the deaf, and encourage youth mentoring.

LESSONS LEARNED

Reflecting on Fort Wayne's successes, Mayor Richard attributes a strong focus on lean principles, committed leadership, and improved financial performance as enablers of positive change. City leaders run the city like a business, utilizing dashboards and other links to the business world to emphasize executive accountability. Data-based decision-making and empowerment of city employees have been the key components of the program's success.[3]

"Fort Wayne has implemented the lean process to improve customer service and increase the effectiveness of city government processes. The use of Six Sigma demonstrates the city's commitment to innovation and continuous improvement. Mayor Richard's vision to bring a high-powered private sector program to government has not only enhanced services for Fort Wayne citizens, but has also created a culture of renewed enthusiasm among employees to do their jobs better."[4]

REFERENCES

1. http://www.cityoffortwayne.org. Accessed March 3, 2006.
2. Greg Meszaros and Maria Gomez-Espino, "Enhancing Public Service Through Lean Six Sigma Process Improvement Techniques," 2005.
3. Graham Richard, "Building a High-Performance City: How the City of Fort Wayne Used Lean Six Sigma to Improve Services and Reduce Costs."
4. http://www.cityoffortwayne.org.

Appendix C

Case Study #2: The Bank of America/FleetBoston Merger—Ensuring Customer Delight with Lean Six Sigma

INTRODUCTION

The two main drivers of Bank of America's strategy
continue to be the customer . . . and the customer.
Our strategy is to attract more customers, retain more
of those we have and deepen relationships with both
groups. In late 2003, we reached a definitive agreement
to acquire FleetBoston Financial. This combination
creates a bank unrivaled in America's fastest-growing
and wealthiest markets. Making certain our customers
have the right products and services to meet their
banking and investment needs will drive our strategy.

Ken Lewis, CEO, Bank of America
The Banker, January 2004

The above quote from Bank of America's chief executive officer demonstrates the firm's vision for growth and prosperity and even more importantly, its steadfast commitment to its customers. While the merger with FleetBoston represented a significant and strategic business opportunity, Bank of America's senior leader also recognized that, if not properly managed, the acquisition could potentially have catastrophic affects on customer relationships. For this reason, Bank of America engineered a quality-based initiative to ensure that once the merger was complete, customers would be satisfied, even delighted, with the resulting products and services. They called this initiative Design for Growth, an adaptation of Design for Six Sigma (DFSS) as it relates to the banking industry, coupled with additional tools designed to assess customer needs and measure stakeholder impact. Following the merger, a lean enterprise approach was employed to simplify and optimize the combined processes.

THE PREPLAN/DEFINE PHASE

As with all Six Sigma projects, Bank of America's Design for Growth initiative began with defining the project scope, identifying the voice of the customer (VOC), and establishing critical to quality (CTQ) characteristics that would need to be present following the merger to retain and delight its product and service users. As part of its VOC study, Bank of America incorporated vital feedback from primary stakeholders including external customers, bank associates, business partners, communities, and competitors. The resulting perspectives provided a broad and accurate view of all constituents affected by the merger.

Another important component of the define phase was to position the Bank of America brand within the Fleet franchise (that is, establish the value proposition). This was accomplished through the use of a Zaltman Metaphor Elicitation Technique (ZMET) analysis. ZMET is a patented research tool designed to uncover "beliefs and feelings that influence the behavior of consumers and stakeholders."[1] One approach is to measure a subject's responses to visual and audible stimuli to better understand how consumers think and feel about certain products or brand images. The results of the analysis included a list of customers' perceived values connected to Bank of America, which helped guide the design in later stages.

THE MEASURE PHASE

Information gathered from the VOC studies was translated into quantifiable and actionable requirements through the use of Kano analysis, named for Japanese professor Noriaki Kano. First, subject matter experts were used to develop survey questions that were administered to focus groups comprising bank clients from each of the identified market segments and geographic locations. Kano analysis was then used to categorize survey responses into three levels of customer needs: basic (dissatisfiers), performance (satisfiers), and exciters (delighters).

Basic needs are those requirements that are expected in a product or service and if not present result in extreme customer dissatisfaction. Performance needs are generally not expected; however, fulfilling them creates satisfaction. Exciters are new and innovative features that customers do not expect but can lead to high perceptions of quality. Bank of America performed Kano analysis on multiple CTQs across various segments to "minimize dissatisfaction and improve delight."[2]

THE ANALYZE PHASE

"Based on the *measure* phase Kano analysis, an adaptation of SERVQUAL was used to determine key countermeasure areas to manage."[3] This service quality assessment tool was designed by the marketing research team of Berry, Parasuraman, and Zeithaml (PB&Z) and has been used in a wide variety of service industries, including banking. "Through numerous qualitative studies, they evolved a set of five dimensions which have been consistently ranked by customers to be most important for service quality, regardless of service industry."[4] These dimensions are *tangibles, reliability, responsiveness, assurance,* and *empathy.* "The researchers also developed a survey instrument to measure the gap between customers' expectation for excellence and their perception of actual service delivered. The SERVQUAL instrument helps service providers understand both customer expectations and perceptions of specific services, as well as quality improvements over time."[5] Bank of America utilized the SERVQUAL dimensions to assess major impact areas of their business related to services and features, among others. Research conducted by PB&Z has concluded that, regardless of industry, "reliablity is the most important contributor to service quality and tangibles is the least important."[6]

During the *analyze* phase, Bank of America also translated Kano analysis output into actionable tasks using quality function deployment (QFD). Identified CTQs were prioritized into a *house of quality* framework and each characteristic was assessed with recommendations to either keep as is (that is, do nothing), develop a hybrid offering, or convert to a new model.

THE IMPROVE AND CONTROL PHASES

Factors resulting from SERVQUAL analysis represent gaps between customer perceptions and the model post-merger environment. Each of these gaps was evaluated to determine implications to current Bank of America customers, and improvement projects were assigned to close the gaps.

Lean enterprise tools were employed during the transition, with kaizen blitz events planned to simplify merged processes. Process mapping was used to illustrate the interaction of people, processes, and systems in the new structure, as well as to identify and eliminate non-value-added activities. Cycle time reduction techniques were applied to services such as mortgage processing with the goal of delighting customers and minimizing costs. Another important outcome of Bank of America's Design for Growth initiative was an impact assessment performed to address specific customer concerns and ensure that positive attributes were associated with the resulting products and services.

RESULTS

- 196,000 new savings accounts were added in 2004 among previous Fleet customers.

- Bank of America's shares rose 16.9 percent versus a 6.3 percent return for the Philadelphia KBW Bank Index.

- Products per customer increased from 1.9 to 4.1 and are expected to hit 6.4 according to Liam McGee, head of Consumer and Small Business Banking at Bank of America.[7]

- Top 2 box (customer) satisfaction increased to 47.3 percent in the fourth quarter of 2004, an increase of approximately 420,000 customers in just one quarter.

- Customer satisfaction also increased in checking, savings, and credit cards. Satisfaction numbers jumped nearly seven percent for checking products and more than 12 percent for savings products in the fourth quarter of 2004.

- At the same time, customer dissatisfaction dropped to 10.9 percent in the fourth quarter from 14.1 percent in the previous quarter. Dissatisfied customers are those who give the company a five or less on a 10-point scale.

By all counts, Bank of America is on its way to a successful merger. The amount of customer churn is extremely low and, in fact, business in the old FleetBoston franchise has actually grown."[8] When asked to identify contributors to the merger's success, Chief Marketing Officer Cathy Bessan commented, "It was a combination of the customer-based research as well as deep technical understanding that enabled us to lay out our plan."[9] Bank of America applied Six Sigma to "develop a more thorough understanding of customer expectations. Additionally, Six Sigma methods were applied to improve merger execution and risk mitigation."[10]

ENDNOTES

1. OZA Overview, http://www.olsonzaltman.com/oza/zmet.html.
2. Rick Otero. "Engineering Customer Delight with Six Sigma: Design for Growth applied to the Bank of America and Fleet Boston Merger," master's degree thesis, Clarkson University, 2005.
3. Ibid.
4. Danuta A. Nitecki, "SERVQUAL: Measuring Service Quality in Academic Libraries," http://www.arl.org/newsltr/191/servqual.html.
5. Ibid.
6. Ibid.
7. Dean Foust. "BofA's Happy Surprise: Consumer Chief McGee's Sweeping Makeover of Fleet's Branches Is a Success." *Business Week,* May 6, 2005. http://businessweek.com/magazine/content/05_06/b3919105_mz020.htm.
8. Otero, "Engineering Customer Delight."
9. Constantine Von Hoffman. "The Art (and Science) of the Deal," *CMO Magazine,* May 2005.
10. Otero, "Engineering Customer Delight."

Appendix D

Case Study #3:
Eastman Kodak Company—
A Manufacturing
Success Story

In order to stay competitive, aggressive goals to improve safety, quality, and productivity and to reduce inventories are handed out each year. One approach to meeting these goals is to look at current value stream maps that highlight opportunities and then formulate a plan to meet the business unit goals.

This is a success story about one of those plans in 2005. The seal strength of one particular product was the opportunity. Poor seal strength resulted in customer complaints, was very high on the Pareto analysis of waste, and also caused a significant disruption to product flow.

After some discussion, the leadership team agreed to use a Six Sigma project conducted in kaizen fashion to tackle this opportunity. This approach had already been used successfully for several projects at Kodak: After initial preparatory work, a one-week kaizen event is conducted to address the define–measure–analyze phases of the Six Sigma DMAIC process. During the following three to four weeks, data collection and analysis required to complete the *analyze* phase is conducted, and some designed experiments might be run. Then a second one-week kaizen event is held to address the *improve* phase. By the end of the week, a kaizen newspaper is created for follow-up activities to be completed within the next 60 days. These activities bring closure to the improve phase and address the *control* phase of DMAIC. This particular project was deemed suitable for this approach for the following reasons:

- Kaizen creates the sense of urgency to make change

- The disciplined approach of kaizen was needed to achieve the expected results

- The use of Six Sigma tools is critical in the data-driven approach to better understand and solve the problem.

The first task in our success story was to assemble a diverse kaizen team that consisted of Black Belts, operators, mechanics, quality technicians, a lean manufacturing facilitator, and outside eyes. With very strong management backing, the effort began with a five-day kaizen event that focused on defining the problem in great detail and collecting the mountain of data that helped describe the current state. Tools used during the first one-week event included:

- Process mapping to fully understand the current process and to define key inputs and outputs

- Brainstorming to identify the initial eight to 10 input variables for a screening experiment

- Data gathering to validate the problem; some of the results reinforced initial premises while others presented some surprises

The second one-week kaizen was scheduled for four weeks later. This allowed ample time for data analysis in the interim. Specific tools used in that time period were:

- Complete evaluation of the current measurement system. The data showed that the current system was inadequate and needed to be improved.

- Design of experiments to better understand the influence and interaction of the various equipment and material parameters. These also helped identify optimal values.

- Capability analysis of the current process to determine the expected level of performance.

- Control charting to monitor process performance over time and assess stability.

- Fishbone diagram/Pareto voting to identify and evaluate key areas for improvement.

In this same time period the following lean manufacturing tools were used:

- *PDCA*. Create a plan, do the plan, check or verify whether the expected results were achieved, and then take action. If the expected results are not achieved, a new plan is created.

- *Gemba.* Go to where the work is being done. Don't assume that you know; instead, go see!

The second week of kaizen focused on making changes to improve seal strength. Some change was made to improve the current condition but the team recognized that more time was needed in the evaluation phase, and the work continued beyond the second week. A kaizen newspaper captured the problems and planned countermeasures, along with identifying the responsible person and a due date for completion of the item. A kaizen sub-team met daily for 30 minutes with very stringent standard work to review only the items that were at risk of not being completed on time. In hindsight, these meetings were instrumental in contributing to the success of the overall effort.

Within the ensuing months the team implemented the countermeasures. Waste was reduced by over 30 percent, with an accompanying significant reduction in flow disruptions. This translated into significant financial savings for the operation. And best of all, for the six months following the event there were zero customer complaints!

The authors would like to acknowledge Albert Menting, Project Leader, and Stephen Eckert, Black Belt, both of Eastman Kodak Company, for this case study.

Contributing Authors

Robert M. Meisel is principal consultant with RMM Quality Consulting, specializing in the training and application of Six Sigma and lean methodology as well as basic problem solving, root cause analysis, and change management. Prior to that Bob spent over 30 years at Eastman Kodak Company in various quality management positions. Bob is a Fellow of ASQ and is chair of the ASQ Quality Management Division's Lean Six Sigma Technical Committee. He is a certified Master Black Belt and is an ASQ certified manager of quality/organization excellence and certified quality engineer. Bob has a master's and bachelor's degree in chemical engineering, and a master's degree in applied and mathematical statistics. He can be contacted at bob@rmmqc.com.

Steven J. Babb is CEO of REAL Balanced Solutions, Inc. and a principal consultant with Business Consulting Group, LLC. Steve is a senior member of ASQ, a member of the ASQ Quality Management Division's Lean Six Sigma Technical Committee, and chair of the St. Petersburg–Tampa ASQ section. Steve is an ASQ certified manager of quality/organizational excellence, quality engineer, and quality auditor. He is a Master Black Belt, registered professional engineer in North Carolina, and NADCAP aerospace accreditation auditor. Steve serves on advisory boards for several entrepreneurial companies. Steve has a master's and bachelor's degree in chemical engineering. He can be contacted at sbabb@REALBalancedSolutions.com.

Steven F. Marsh is director of the engineering and global operations management graduate program at Clarkson University. He gained over 15 years experience as a quality professional in the medical device, electronics, and aluminum industries. Steve is a senior member of ASQ, a member of the ASQ Quality Management Division's Lean Six Sigma Technical Committee, an ASQ certified quality engineer, and is currently pursuing a certified Six Sigma Black Belt. He holds both an MS in engineering and manufacturing management and a BS in interdisciplinary engineering and management from Clarkson, and earned an AS in engineering science from SUNY Canton. He can be contacted at smarsh@clarkson.edu.

James P. Schlichting is a project manager in engineering and quality assurance at Abbott Laboratories—Diagnostic Division. James is a senior member of AIChE, IEEE, and ASQ, and a member of the ASQ Quality Management Division's Lean Six Sigma Technical Committee. James has six ASQ certifications: Six Sigma Black Belt, quality engineer, reliability engineer, software quality engineer, quality auditor, and manager of quality/organizational excellence. James is a licensed professional engineer in Illinois. James has an MS in chemical engineering, an MBA, and an MS in management information systems. He can be contacted at james.schlichting@abbott.com.

Index

A

American Society for Quality
  Quality Management Division,
    xi–xii
  as resource for Lean Six Sigma
    implementation, 46
  Six Sigma Belt certifications, 60
appraisal costs, 35
  items, 68

B

balance sheet, 30
Bank of America/FleetBoston, Lean
    Six Sigma implementation
    (Appendix C), 75–79
benchmarking, 65–66
benefits, of Lean Six Sigma
    implementation, 49
Black Belts, Six Sigma, 20–21
  training, 60
breakthrough goals, in Lean Six
    Sigma implementation, 54
business performance, measures of,
    28

C

cash flow statement, 31
Champions, Six Sigma, 18
  training, 60
colleges, as resource for Lean Six
    Sigma implementation, 46
communication, in Lean Six Sigma
    implementation, 23, 59
consultants, as resource for Lean Six
    Sigma implementation, 46
conveyance, as type of waste, 4
  economics of, 32–33
correction, as type of waste, 3
  economics of, 35
cost of goods sold (COGS), 29
cost of poor quality. *See* cost of
    quality
cost of quality (COQ), 35–38
  categories, 35
  and improvement strategy, 37
  and sigma quality levels, 16
cost of quality items (Appendix A),
    67–70
cultural shift, required for Lean
    Six Sigma implementation,
    46–47

customers, in Lean Six Sigma
  implementation, 50–51

D

dashboards, in Lean Six Sigma
  implementation, 54–55
defects, definition under Six Sigma,
  14
DMAIC (define–measure–analyze–
  improve–control) methodology,
  17–18

E

Eastman Kodak Company, Lean
  Six Sigma implementation
  (Appendix D), 81–83
economics of waste, 32–35
executive commitment
  in Lean Six Sigma, 23
  in Lean Six Sigma
    implementation, 53–54
executive sponsors, in Six Sigma,
  18
external failure costs, 35
  items, 69–70

F

finance
  concepts, 29–31
  involvement in valuing projects,
    43
financial analysts, in Six Sigma, 21
financial measures, 28–29
five principles, of lean, 2–3
5S, 11–12
FleetBoston/Bank of America, Lean
  Six Sigma implementation
  (Appendix C), 75–79
Fort Wayne, Indiana, Lean Six Sigma
  implementation (Appendix B),
  71–74
forums, as resource for Lean Six
  Sigma implementation,
  46, 65

G

gemba, 83
goals, breakthrough, in Lean Six
  Sigma implementation, 54
Green Belts, Six Sigma, 21
  training, 60
gross profit (margin), 29–30

H

hard savings, versus soft savings,
  31–32
hidden costs of quality, 36
hidden factory, 3

I

improvement, contribution to
  financials, 31–32
improvement initiatives
  guidelines on valuing, 42–43
  hypothetical example, 38–42
  successful, example, 38
improvement projects, guidelines on
  valuing, 42–43
improvement results, expressing in
  language of managers, 27
internal failure costs, 35
  items, 68–69
inventory, as type of waste, 4
  economics of, 33
ISO 9000, and Lean Six Sigma
  implementation, 47–48

J

jidoka, 12
just in time, 12

K

kaizen, 10–11, 81–83
Kano analysis, 76–77
knowledge, as critical success factor
  for Lean Six Sigma, 24

L

language of business/managers
  expressing improvement results
    in, 27
  leveraging, in Lean Six Sigma
    implementation, 54
lean, 2–13
  concepts, in Lean Six Sigma
    implementation, 57
  early concepts, 1
  five principles of, 2–3
  similarity with Six Sigma, 1–2
  versus Six Sigma or lean and Six
    Sigma, 21–22, 49–50
lean enterprise/company,
    characteristics of, 2–3
Lean Sigma. *See* Lean Six Sigma
Lean Six Sigma, 2, 22
  necessity of, 24–25
  preparing for, 23–25
Lean Six Sigma enterprise, becoming,
    64
Lean Six Sigma implementation,
    45–66
  Bank of America/FleetBoston
    merger (Appendix C),
    75–79
  commitment involved, 46–47
  Eastman Kodak Company
    (Appendix D), 81–83
  Fort Wayne, Indiana (Appendix
    B), 71–74
  getting started, 49–65
  growing your success, 65–66
  resources available, 45–46
  sharing your successes, 66
  six phases of, 51–53
lean tools, 9–13

M

management commitment
  in Lean Six Sigma, 23
  in Lean Six Sigma
    implementation, 53–54
management sponsors, in Six Sigma,
    18
Master Black Belts, Six Sigma, 20

measurement systems analysis
  (MSA), in DMAIC, 17
measures
  of business performance, 28
  financial, 28–29
metrics, in Lean Six Sigma
  implementation, 54–56
motion, as type of waste, 3–4
  economics of, 33–34
movement, unnecessary, as type of
  waste, 4
  economics of, 32–33

N

networks, as resource for Lean Six
  Sigma implementation, 46, 65
nonmanufacturing organizations
  alternatives for, 65
  and Lean Six Sigma
    implementation, 48, 71–74
non-value-adding activities, as
  percentage of total cycle time,
  7–8

O

one-piece flow, 13
organizational culture, and Lean Six
  Sigma implementation, 46–47,
  48–49
overprocessing, as type of waste, 4
  economics of, 34–35
overproduction, as type of waste, 4
  economics of, 34

P

plan–do–check–act (PDCA) cycle,
  9–10
planning, in Lean Six Sigma
  implementation, 51–53
prevention costs, 35
  items, 67–68
process owners, in Six Sigma, 20
processing, as type of waste, 4
  economics of, 34–35

profit and loss (P&L) statement,
29–30
project charters, 58
project funnel, 58
project leader, skills, 58
project management, in Lean Six
Sigma implementation, 53
project selection, in Lean Six Sigma
implementation, 50, 57–58
project tracking software, 66
projects, in Lean Six Sigma, 23–24
guidelines for, 61–63
guidelines on valuing, 42–43
hypothetical example, 61–63

R

readiness, organizational, in Lean Six
Sigma implementation, 51
repair and rework, as waste, 3
economics of, 35
resources, for Lean Six Sigma
implementation, 45–46

S

scrap, as type of waste, 3
selling, general, and administrative
(SG&A) expenses, 30
SERVQUAL assessment tool, 77
seven types of waste, 3–5
economics of, 32–35
sigma quality level, 14–16, 57
SIPOC model, of process, 65
six phases of Lean Six Sigma
implementation, 51–53
Six Sigma, 13–21
goal of, 13
history, 1
versus lean or Six Sigma and lean,
21–22, 49–50
methodology, 17–21
metric, 14–16
philosophy, 13–14
similarity with lean concepts, 1–2
smaller organizations, alternatives for,
64–65
SMART metrics, 56

soft savings
versus hard savings, 31–32
valuing, 43
software, project tracking, 66
standard deviation (σ), 13
standard work, 12
suppliers, in Lean Six Sigma
implementation, 50–51

T

team members, in Six Sigma, 21
tools, lean versus Six Sigma, 61
Toyota Production System, 1
training, in Lean Six Sigma
implementation, 47, 59–61

U

universities, as resource for Lean Six
Sigma implementation, 46

V

value stream analysis, 5–9
value stream mapping, 5–9
four stages, 7
value-adding activities, as percentage
of total cycle time, 7–8
variation, and Six Sigma, 13–14
visual management, 12

W

waiting, as type of waste, 5
economics of, 34
waste
definition, 2
economics of seven types, 32–35
types of, 3–5
Welch, Jack, 13

Z

Zaltman Metaphor Elicitation
Technique (ZMET) analysis, 76